INNOVATIVE MINDS

Stephen Hawking
SOLVING THE MYSTERIES OF THE UNIVERSE

Ron Cole

RSVP

RAINTREE
STECK-VAUGHN
PUBLISHERS
The Steck-Vaughn Company

Austin, Texas

Acknowledgments
The publisher would like to acknowledge Professor Michael Zeller, Yale University Physics Department, for his expert review of the manuscript.

Published by Raintree Steck-Vaughn Publishers, an imprint of Steck-Vaughn Company.

Series created by Blackbirch Graphics
Series Editor: Tanya Lee Stone
Editor: Lisa Clyde Nielsen
Associate Editor: Elizabeth M. Taylor
Production/Design Editor: Calico Harington

Raintree Steck-Vaughn Staff
Editors: Shirley Shalit, Kathy DeVico
Project Manager: Lyda Guz

Library of Congress Cataloging-in-Publication Data
Cole, Ron.
    Stephen Hawking : solving the mysteries of the universe / by Ron Cole.
        p.   cm. — (Innovative minds)
    Includes bibliographical references and index.
    Summary: Discusses the life and work of the brilliant physicist who has overcome the challenges of a life-threatening disease to become one of the foremost scientists of the twentieth century.
    ISBN 0-8172-4401-8
    1. Hawking, S. W. (Stephen W.)—Juvenile literature. 2. Physicists—Great Britain—Biography—Juvenile literature. [1. Hawking, S. W. (Stephen W.) 2. Physicists. 3. Physically handicapped.]   I. Title. II. Series.
QC16.H33C65   1997
530'.092—dc20
[B]   96-18931
                                                        CIP
                                                         AC

Printed in the United States of America
1 2 3 4 5 6 7 8 9 0 LB 00 99 98 97 96

Table of Contents

Stephen Hawking has fascinated millions of people around the world with his continuing efforts to understand the cosmos.

CHAPTER ONE

THE
CURIOUS
INTELLECT

In England, at Oxford University, despite—or perhaps because of—his lack of effort, Stephen Hawking quickly became known as a brilliant student. Robert Berman, his physics instructor, described Hawking as the most intelligent student he had ever had.

Once in the early 1960s, Berman assigned four students, including Hawking, 13 extremely difficult problems in the scientific field of physics (which studies the physical laws of nature) to try to solve by the next week's class.

The three other students worked hard on the problems all week. By the morning of the class, one of the students had completed a single problem. The other two, working together, had completed only one and a half problems. Stephen Hawking, however, had solved all of the first ten problems on the day they were due—in just three hours, between 9:00 A.M. and noon!

This incident caused Derek Powney, one of the three other physics students, to comment that Hawking was so smart that he was not only in a different league; he was on a different planet!

In 1962, at the very beginning of his scientific career, Stephen Hawking developed an incurable disabling disease; his doctors told him that he would probably die within a few years. Today, in his mid-fifties, although he is paralyzed and is able to "talk" only through the use of a finger-controlled computer, he is still actively seeking what he calls a "theory of everything" to explain the universe.

Over the past three decades, Stephen Hawking's work in the field of cosmology—the branch of astronomy that studies the overall structure, size, age, history, and possible fate of the universe—has firmly established his place high among the ranks of the greatest minds of the twentieth century. Other scientists have recognized his many contributions to cosmological theory by giving him most of science's highest awards. In addition, he has enjoyed perhaps the greatest popular fame of any living scientist.

Hawking achieved this fame in part through his immensely popular book on cosmology, *A Brief History of Time*, which was published in 1988. His celebrity, however, is mainly due to his dramatic and incredible triumph over profound physical adversity. Hawking has achieved this triumph with the help and devotion of his loved ones, friends, and even total strangers, but especially through his own brilliance and determination.

A Normal Childhood in Abnormal Times

Stephen William Hawking was born in Oxford, England, on January 8, 1942, exactly 300 years after the death of Galileo, the founder of modern physical science. At the time of Hawking's birth, the tide of World War II, which had raged since September 1939, was just starting to turn in Great Britain's favor. In December 1941, the United States, with its vast industrial and military might, had joined Great Britain and the Soviet Union in their struggle against Germany, Japan, and Italy. However, the Luftwaffe—the German Air Force—was still bombing London and the rest of southern England almost nightly.

Germany had agreed not to bomb Great Britain's university cities of Cambridge and Oxford if, in return, Great Britain would not bomb Germany's university cities of Heidelberg and Göttingen. So Stephen Hawking's parents, who lived in the London suburb of Highgate, decided for safety's sake that their first child should be born in Oxford.

Stephen's father, Frank, was one of seven children in a middle-class British family. Frank, however, managed to attend Oxford University, a world-renowned university then attended mainly by children of the wealthy. Having received several scholarships and prizes, he graduated in 1927 with "First Class Honours." In 1933 Frank Hawking received his medical degree. After doing research in tropical medicine, he went to East Africa in 1937 to study tropical diseases. When war with Germany broke out in September 1939, he took a ship back to England. Although he volunteered there for military service, he was told that he would be more valuable to England as a medical researcher.

Stephen Hawking's mother, Isobel, was born in Glasgow, Scotland. She was the second oldest of seven children of a family physician and his wife. At a time when very few women went to college, Isobel's parents made the sacrifices that were necessary to send her to Oxford University in the 1930s. Once there, Isobel studied philosophy, politics, and economics.

After she graduated from the university, Isobel held a series of jobs that she did not like. The one that she disliked the most was a position as a tax inspector. Eventually, Isobel became a secretary at a medical-research institute, a position for which she was extremely overqualified. She and Frank Hawking met there.

Isobel and Frank had been married for several years when Stephen, their first child, was born. When the baby was just two weeks old, Isobel took him back to the Hawkings' Victorian-style house located in the London suburb of Highgate. They had been able to buy the house at a bargain price, because many Londoners feared that German bombing would level the city. (The house survived the war, though its back windows were blown out when a German V-2 rocket destroyed a neighbor's house.)

In 1943, when Stephen was 18 months old, his sister Mary was born. Another sister, Philippa, was born in 1946, when Stephen was nearly five.

As a young child, Stephen was slow in learning how to read. However, he was always very interested in finding out how things worked. To this end, for example, he took clocks and radios apart to observe the arrangement and movement of their parts. By the time he was eight or nine, Stephen already wanted to become a scientist. He felt that science could answer all his questions about the world around him.

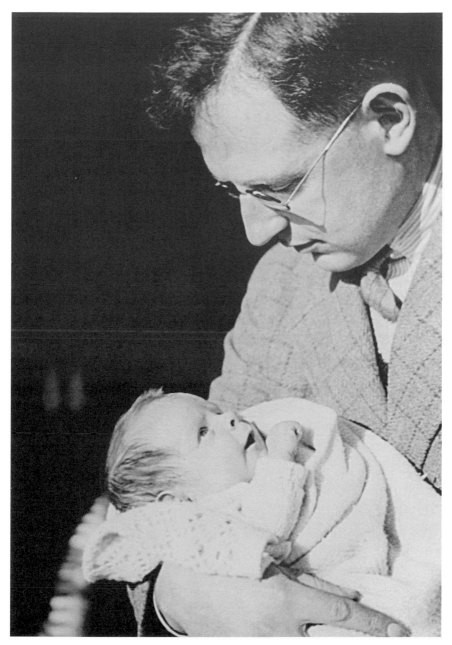

Stephen, less than one month old, is held by his father,
Frank Hawking. The first of the children of Frank and
his wife, Isobel, Stephen was born during World War II.

The Eccentric Hawking Family

After World War II ended, Stephen's father became head of the Division of Parasitology at the National Institute for Medical Research. As part of his job, he spent the first three or four months of nearly every year in Africa, doing field-work in tropical medicine.

In 1950 the National Institute moved its quarters from Hampstead, near Highgate, to a newly constructed facility in Mill Hill, on the northern edge of London. To be closer to Frank's work, the family moved 20 miles north to St. Albans, a small cathedral city.

The Hawking family's new home was a large and once-elegant Victorian house that had fallen into disrepair. Stephen's parents could afford only to purchase the house and pay for some major repairs necessary to make it livable; they did not have enough money to get the house into perfect condition. As a result, the Hawkings constantly lived with broken greenhouse windows, peeling wallpaper, holes in plaster walls, frayed carpets, old furniture, inadequate lighting, a rotting front porch, and a collapsing front fence. Although every room contained a fireplace, only a single fire was kept going to heat the entire house. Stephen's brother Edward, who was adopted as an infant in 1955, later reported that frost often covered the inside walls of his room on winter mornings.

Stephen's L-shaped bedroom had once been a maid's room. To Stephen, it had the advantage that he could climb through the window onto the roof of the bicycle shed and then easily reach the ground. He boasted that he knew 11 different ways of getting out of the house.

Both Isobel and Frank Hawking encouraged their children to be intellectually curious and to explore the world around them. Here, young Stephen guides a sailboat.

The shabbiness of the house was just one of many things that gave the Hawkings a reputation for eccentricity in the eyes of their neighbors. They kept bees in their basement. Books were stacked two-deep on all of the bookshelves and filled every other available space. Any space not taken up by books contained a painting or some unusual article that Frank Hawking had brought back from his travels. Friends who stayed for dinner reported that, while they were talking with Stephen, the rest of the family would be reading books at the dinner table.

Frank stuttered, and Stephen and other members of the family often stammered or spoke so fast that no one could understand them. Stephen's friends came to call his speech "Hawkingese." Some people thought that the Hawkings were so intelligent that their speech could not keep pace with their thoughts.

At a time when the wealthy owned most of the cars in Great Britain, the Hawkings drove around in a used, open-air taxicab. The children played games around a table in the back as the car "raced" along—at its top speed of 40 miles per hour. The Hawkings also kept an old, brightly colored trailer on the south coast of Great Britain. For many years, they stayed in it for several weeks during their summer vacations.

Intellectual curiosity and exploration of the world were strongly encouraged in the Hawking family. According to Isobel Hawking, Stephen was a "self-educator" from the time he was very young. He just seemed to soak up information. She routinely took Stephen to the Science Museum at South Kensington. She would leave him to explore it while she took his sisters to museums of interest to them. She also took Stephen to political rallies in support of nuclear disarmament (a movement of people against the manufacture and use of nuclear weapons). Perhaps as a result, he has continued to be interested in politics and strongly sympathetic to the political left.

Frank Hawking was a shy person, mainly concerned about his job and about supporting his family on his modest income. Since his job-related trips abroad kept him away from the family for several months each year, Isobel played the major role in bringing up the children. But Stephen considered his father, as a scientific researcher, the greater influence in his life. He felt that going into some sort of scientific research was a natural thing to do when he grew up, because he modeled himself after his father.

It was not just as a role model that Frank Hawking stimulated Stephen's interest in science. He involved all of his children in scientific activities. For instance, because fireworks were expensive, Frank taught the children how to make their own. In this way, Stephen learned a lot about chemistry, including the chemicals needed to produce the different colors in the exploding fireworks. Stephen and his father also took nature hikes and recorded the species of plants they observed.

At Frank's laboratory at the National Institute, Stephen enjoyed looking through the microscope, but he worried about people's exposure to the mosquitoes flying around in the insect house. (His concern was merited, because, in the interest of research, the laboratory scientists had infected the insects with tropical diseases.) Stephen's father at first also helped him with mathematics, but the boy's skill soon surpassed his father's. Finally, and perhaps most significantly for Stephen's future career, his father taught the children how to use the family telescope to look at the stars in the nighttime sky.

Studies in St. Albans

When he was eight years old, Stephen began attending the High School for Girls, in St. Albans, which accepted male students up to the age of ten. But after he had been there for only one term, his father took an unusually long trip to Africa. During the time that Frank Hawking was away, the rest of the family, including Stephen, lived in a village on the Spanish island of Majorca. His mother visited with a school friend of hers who was married to the famous poet Robert Graves. While they were in Majorca, Stephen shared a tutor with Graves's son William.

Once back at St. Albans, Stephen attended another school for a year. He then passed the admissions test for the local public school (what Americans call private school) for boys in St. Albans. The school had a reputation for academic excellence. By getting a high score on a nation-wide intelligence test for children, Stephen won a full scholarship. At age ten, he was one of 90 boys who began their studies as "senior students" at St. Albans School on September 23, 1952.

The senior-school program at St. Albans was roughly similar to junior high followed by high school in the United States. During their five forms (grades) as senior students, the boys studied a wide range of subjects. They then took "Ordinary (O) Level" examinations to test their mastery of this material. Students who did well typically prepared for university admission by taking two years of "Advanced Level Courses" in a few subjects. The courses at this level were similar to the advanced placement courses that exist in American high schools.

Stephen sits on a horse during a vacation. His friends nicknamed him "Einstein" when they realized how brilliant he was.

Because of his high test scores, Stephen was placed in the "A Stream." This was the highest of the three levels for each form. At the end of the first form, the A Stream was limited to the top 20 students. Stephen just made the cut, ranking 18th.

Stephen's teachers in the third form recognized him as bright, but they never ranked him above the middle of the A Stream. Perhaps this is because his fellow students were also very smart. Stephen's terrible handwriting and the general untidiness of his homework, however, may have also hurt his academic ranking.

Stephen's classmates regarded him as more intelligent than the teachers did. They even gave him the nickname "Einstein," after the brilliant physicist Albert Einstein. By his third year at St. Albans School, Stephen and a small group of close friends had earned the status of the brightest group of the class.

Students at St. Albans were usually assigned three hours of homework each night during the school week. On Saturday, there were classes in the morning, and students were expected to participate in sports in the afternoon. Homework had to be done over the weekend, too.

Despite this heavy workload, Stephen and his friends found time to relax and have fun. They enjoyed taking long bicycle rides in the countryside around St. Albans. They often read and talked about the works of leading British writers. They also listened to classical music on the radio and went to classical music concerts held at Albert Hall in London. In 1957 Stephen built a record player out of inexpensive spare parts. He used this to listen to the long-playing classical records that had just appeared in Great Britain.

With his closest school friend, John McClenahan, Stephen built model boats and airplanes that he controlled by radio, using circuits of his own design and construction. Stephen and another of his group, Roger Ferneyhaugh, spent much time inventing and playing complicated board games.

Roger, who had artistic talent, designed and made the game boards and pieces. Stephen invented the rules of the games, a talent that was an outgrowth of his interest in knowing how things worked and how to control them.

Exploring the Meaning of Life

By the time Stephen and his friends were in the third form, in 1954–1955, they had begun to discuss religion, mysticism, magic, and the meaning of life. Their discussions about religion stemmed from a visit that the American evangelist Billy Graham had made to Great Britain. Although some in the group actively embraced Christianity, Hawking displayed a detached attitude toward the religious discussions. Some of these discussions, however, may have triggered his interest in cosmology, because he began thinking about the origin of the universe. He heard that some cosmologists thought that the universe was expanding. However, at the time, he thought that "an essentially unchanging and everlasting universe seemed so much more natural."

Despite Stephen's cautious, if not skeptical, attitude toward religion, he won the school's prize for religious studies at the end of the third form. He was thoroughly familiar with the Bible, because his father had read Bible stories to him since he was a young child. Moreover, his family routinely had debates on different religious topics, which his father encouraged.

After Stephen and his group of friends had discussed Christianity, they turned their attention to topics lumped under the general category of extrasensory perception (ESP). Believers in ESP claimed that people's minds could

GALILEO

Born in Pisa, Italy, on February 15, 1564, Galileo Galilei was the first person to describe telescopic observations of the heavens, in his work *The Starry Messenger* (1610). Using a telescope only as powerful as today's binoculars, Galileo had observed spots on the Sun,* mountains on the Moon, and several moons orbiting the planet Jupiter. These observations showed that the previously accepted description of the heavens was inaccurate, and they encouraged Galileo to publish a strong argument supporting the views of the Polish astronomer Nicolaus Copernicus (1473–1543).

In his book *On the Revolutions of Heavenly Spheres*, published the year of his death, Copernicus had shocked Europe by challenging the traditional view of Earth's place in the cosmos. The Roman Catholic Church and astronomers of the time held that the Earth was immovable and in the center of the universe, and that the Sun orbited the Earth. This theory had been formulated 1,400 years earlier by the Greek astronomer Ptolemy. Copernicus suggested instead that the Earth rotated daily about its axis while making a yearly orbit around the Sun.

The Catholic Church, which was then the most influential and most powerful institution in Europe, forbade any public defense of these revolutionary Copernican views. Church authorities forced Galileo to publicly deny the Copernican views. And, as punishment for his challenge to Church teachings, they sentenced him to life imprisonment. However, due to Galileo's poor health, the Church allowed him to serve his time under house arrest. Thus, Galileo was confined to his house for the last nine years of his life.

While he was under house arrest, however, Galileo wrote his most important scientific work, *Discourses Concerning Two New Sciences* (1638). In this work, he brilliantly combined mathematics and experimental observation to provide the foundation for the modern theory of moving bodies. Galileo died on January 8, 1642—exactly 300 years to the day before Stephen Hawking was born.

*It is extremely dangerous to look directly at the Sun—especially through binoculars or a telescope.

Galileo Galilei was arrested for saying
publicly that the Earth orbits the Sun.

receive information that did not come through the senses, and that people could affect objects simply by thinking about them. Stephen was an avid reader of science fiction, much of which involved ESP. He found ESP to be a more interesting topic than religion, because he thought that experiments could prove or disprove the claims of ESP supporters. He and his friends tried to see if they could influence the roll of dice by mental power. They lost interest in ESP, however, after they attended a lecture by a scientist who had examined ESP experiments conducted by psychologists at Duke University in the United States. The lecturer thoroughly convinced them that effects that suggested the existence of ESP occurred only in sloppy experiments. When scientists conducted careful, well-designed experiments, the lecturer said, no one seemed to have ESP.

A Scientific Career Begins

In the fall of 1957, after completing the five forms required for senior students, Stephen began two years as an Advanced Level student to prepare to apply to a university. From his early teenage years, he had wanted to study physics, the most basic science. He also had a deep interest in astronomy and mathematics.

In order to be ready to study physics and/or mathematics at the university level, Stephen wanted to take Mathematics, Physics, and Further (higher-level) Mathematics as his Advanced Level courses. His father, however, thought that a university degree in mathematics was too impractical. He believed that Stephen's career would be limited by it, that only teaching jobs would be available to a mathematician.

Frank Hawking argued in favor of a career in medicine, but Stephen was dead set against studying biology, which would have been necessary for following his father's hopes. Stephen did not consider biology a truly fundamental, or basic, science, and it was not a very highly thought of course at school. As a compromise, Stephen took chemistry classes along with physics and a small amount of mathematics; his father felt that learning more chemistry would help Stephen keep his scientific options open.

In spring 1958, Stephen helped to design a computer that the school's Mathematical Society built. In Great Britain, only the Ministry of Defence and a few universities had computers, which in those days were extremely expensive, room-size devices. Stephen's group used parts from discarded telephone switching systems to make their Logical Uniselector Computing Engine (LUCE). Although LUCE could only answer a few questions of a particular type of logic, the group's accomplishment got them a write-up in the local St. Albans newspaper. The following year, the group improved LUCE so that it could perform addition.

Stephen lived with the family of a primary-school friend, Simon Humphrey, during his last year at St. Albans. The rest of Stephen's family drove, in the first new car they had ever bought, from France to India, where Stephen's father was to work in an exchange program with some Indian institutions. Stephen stayed behind because his studies could not be interrupted.

Stephen traveled to Oxford University in spring 1959 to take the school's difficult entrance exams. Over a 2-day period, he was given 12 hours of written examinations on mathematics, physics, and world politics. He also went through tough interviews and oral exams.

Ten days after he returned to St. Albans, Stephen received the good news that he was to come back for a second interview. He had received almost perfect scores on his physics examinations and had done nearly as well on the others. Shortly after his second interview, University College of Oxford University accepted Stephen Hawking and awarded him a scholarship that paid part of his expenses. University College, which his father had attended at Oxford, had been Stephen's first choice.

THE STUDENT'S LIFE AT OXFORD

Oxford University consists of about 30 colleges scattered throughout the city of Oxford. The university was founded in the twelfth century A.D., and the city contains buildings of every architectural period from the Middle Ages to the present. University College, Oxford's oldest college, was founded in 1249. Like most of the colleges, its buildings surround a rectangular open space called a quad. Stephen Hawking lived in a room in one of the college's halls.

The program that British university students take is quite different from that taken by American college students. In the United States, college students graduate after they have passed 30 to 60 courses (depending on whether the college has two academic semesters or three academic quarters per year), and Americans typically take these courses over a period of four or more years. At the university level, British students take a specialized program in a particular academic area, similar to that taken by graduate students at American universities. At Oxford, students take their only crucial examinations at the end of the first and third years of

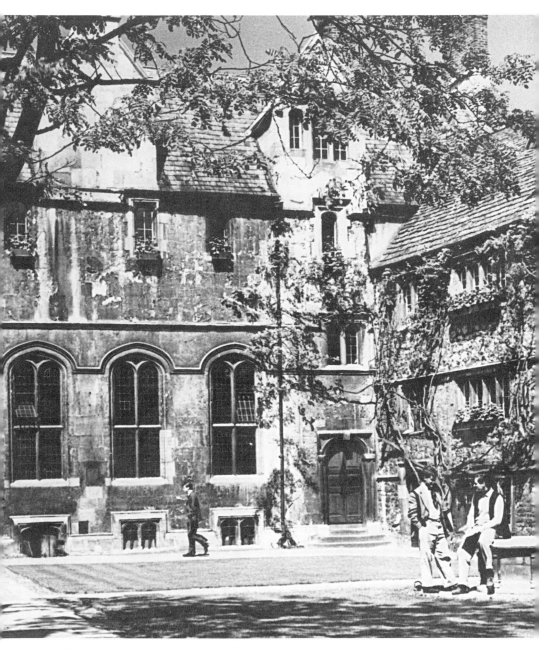

Oxford University is renowned for its architecture. Here,
part of the St. Edmond Hall quadrangle as it was in 1958,
the year before Hawking arrived at the university.

study. A student's degree depends solely on how well the student does on these Finals.

Students at Oxford University are supposed to prepare for these exams by reading, attending lectures, doing problems and other written assignments, and performing laboratory work. Each of Oxford's colleges has professors, called fellows, who head each of the major subject areas; it is their job to see that the students in their college are making suitable progress in preparing for the final examinations. The fellows assign small groups of the students in a particular subject area to a tutor, with whom the students meet once a week in a tutorial. There they go over the written work that was assigned the week before.

When Stephen started at Oxford, he was just 17. It was a difficult period for him. None of his close friends had yet entered the university. Many of the other students were from the upper classes of British society and had attended one of Great Britain's elite public schools, such as Eton, Harrow, Rugby, or Westminster. They tended not to mingle with students from less prominent schools.

What is more, many of the students had spent several years serving in the military forces before starting college. (Great Britain's military draft ended just months before Hawking reached draft age.) They were older than Stephen and tended to be bound together by their military experience. Perhaps for these reasons, Hawking's first year and a half at Oxford was a lonely time.

In the second half of his second year, however, Stephen joined one of the Oxford rowing crews, which competed in races with crews from other colleges. His light weight—he weighed only 140 pounds—and loud voice made him ideally suited to be a coxswain, the person who steers the boat

During his second year at Oxford University, Stephen (far right) joined a rowing crew as a coxswain.

and tells the rowers when to pull on the oars. Hawking and the rest of the crew practiced every day (often at times when he was supposed to be working in the physics lab). Being a member of the Rowing Club helped Hawking to be accepted by the elite social set, who admired his good sense of humor. He and his new friends liked to drink ale and generally have a good time. By the time he reached his third year at the university, he was thoroughly enjoying student life.

Looking back at his Oxford experience, Hawking once observed that most Oxford University students of the day pretended to have an antiwork attitude, a purposely casual approach to their studies. It was considered all right to be brilliant—but one was not supposed to *appear* to be trying.

Stephen Hawking soon adopted this attitude. By his own estimate, he would work for about an hour a day—in contrast, a truly serious physics student would study for about ten hours a day. Along with many of his fellow students, Hawking seemed bored with the world. Hawking's brilliance, however, shone through regardless of his efforts to appear world-weary.

By the end of his second year at Oxford, Hawking had decided to become a theoretical physicist (a physicist, such as Albert Einstein, who develops theories to explain or predict phenomena). There were several reasons behind this decision. He was not very skillful in laboratory work or interested in scientific observations: He had not been very excited even when he observed a double star—a pair of stars orbiting each other—through a powerful telescope. On the other hand, his mathematical ability could help him discover general principles that could explain the results of many experiments.

Hawking initially considered becoming a physicist who studied elementary particles. However, he thought it unlikely that any theory would be developed soon to explain the large and growing number of subatomic particles. He decided instead to become a cosmologist, mainly because he believed that the cosmos could be explained through a suitable application of Einstein's general theory of relativity.

Hawking had not been athletic as a child, but his physical skills had seemed to improve when he took up rowing and coxswaining. Yet, in his third year at Oxford, he became clumsier; he fell over a few times for no apparent reason.

After graduating from Oxford, Hawking went to Cambridge
University to begin graduate studies in cosmology.

ELEMENTARY-PARTICLE THEORY

In the fifth century B.C., the Greek philosopher Democritus introduced the amazing idea of the existence of the atom—the smallest possible particle of matter. Until the end of the nineteenth century A.D., scientists thought that Democritus's atoms were the so-called atoms of the chemical elements, which they considered to be indivisible.

Between 1880 and 1920, however, scientists discovered that the atoms of the chemical elements consist of even smaller parts—negatively charged electrons orbiting positively charged nuclei. The nuclei, in turn, consist of (positively charged) protons and (electrically neutral) neutrons. (Protons, neutrons, and electrons are the main particles of significance to chemists.) These smaller parts of atoms are called subatomic particles.

After 1930, sophisticated scientific experiments in which subatomic particles were made to collide with one another at extremely high speeds yielded many new kinds of particles. By 1960, physicists had discovered several hundred types of these particles. The scientists grouped these particles into families, much as botanists do with plants, and biologists do with animals.

Yet, starting in the mid-1960s, shortly after Stephen Hawking graduated from Oxford University, a vastly simpler view began to appear. According to today's widely accepted "Standard Model" of particle physics, the truly fundamental particles of matter are six types of "leptons" and six "flavors" (types) of "quarks."

Leptons are weakly interacting, pointlike particles, such as electrons. Quarks, by contrast, are strongly interacting particles that join tightly together to form heavier particles, such as protons and neutrons. Each of these quarks and leptons possesses a corresponding "antiparticle"—that is, a particle of matter that is oppositely charged. Some theorists believe that many of these particles consist of a few types of even more fundamental particles!

Near the end of his third year, Hawking fell down the stairs and bumped his head as he tumbled. The blow caused him to lose his memory for a few hours. He then took the intelligence quotient (IQ) test required for admission into the Mensa society—an organization that accepts as members only people with high IQs—to see if he was still above-average in intelligence. His high score on Mensa's IQ test reassured him that he was.

Despite the indications of a health problem, Hawking did not go to see a doctor. With Final Exams fast approaching, he had other things to think about. Cambridge University had accepted him to do graduate (higher level) research in cosmology. However, he would receive the scholarship he needed only if he received a "first" (the highest level) in his Finals at Oxford.

Nervous and fatigued, Hawking did not win an unqualified first in the written exam, so the examiners next step was to interview him to see which level of degree he should receive. According to his tutor Robert Berman, Hawking did brilliantly at his interview. He also displayed the dry wit for which he is now famous. When asked about his plans, Hawking replied that if they gave him a first-class degree, he would go to Cambridge, but if he received the lesser, second-class degree, he would stay at Oxford. He was awarded a first.

THE
APPRENTICE
COSMOLOGIST

$\int$cientific cosmology is the study of the origin, structure, and space-time relationships of the universe. Until 1923, modern astronomers had assumed that the universe consisted of a single galaxy—our own Milky Way, which is a large, spiral galaxy. The American astronomer Edwin Hubble then overturned this longstanding view by using evidence that was collected through a powerful new telescope at the Mount Wilson Observatory, located in southern California.

Hubble's observations proved that objects, then called "spiral nebulae," were in fact separate galaxies. Like the Milky Way, each of these consisted of billions of stars held

Scientists once thought that our galaxy, the Milky Way (part of which is shown here), was the only galaxy that existed in the entire universe.

together by gravity. The most distant star in the Milky Way is about 80,000 light-years away (one light-year, which is the distance that light travels through space in one year, is approximately 6 trillion miles). In contrast, the Andromeda Galaxy M31, the large spiral galaxy nearest to the Milky Way, is an estimated 2 *million* light-years away!

Edwin Hubble and others observed that the spectra (ranges) of light from most of the galaxies that surround the Milky Way are strongly "red shifted"; that is, they are shifted, or moved, to much longer wavelengths. This means that these surrounding galaxies are moving away from us, and at astonishingly high speeds.

The sizes of these red shifts, and therefore the speeds at which galaxies are moving away, are precisely proportional to the galaxies' distances from us. These speeds are between 35,000 and 70,000 miles per hour for each 1 million light-years' distance that a galaxy is from us.

Most cosmologists now believe that space is expanding equally in all directions, carrying the material objects of the universe along with it. Thus, no matter where an observer is located in the universe, all of the surrounding galaxies are moving away. The general expansion of the universe adds more space between the observer and a galaxy as the galaxy is farther away, which means that galaxies that are far from the observer are moving away from the observer at a faster speed than nearby galaxies are.

To visualize this model of an expanding universe, imagine gluing tiny paper stars on a balloon and then inflating the balloon. When considered from the point of view of each separate star, all of the others would move away as the balloon is expanded, and they move away faster as they become farther apart.

Stephen Hawking

When Stephen Hawking arrived at Cambridge University in 1962, two major rival theories were in use to explain the observed expansion of the universe. The more popular of the two was called the "Big Bang" theory, first proposed in 1929 by the Belgian scientist Georges Lemaître. According to Lamaître's proposal, all of the matter, energy, space, and time of the universe had once been concentrated in an extremely small volume. At the moment of the explosion known as the Big Bang, all of these elements suddenly expanded violently outward in all directions. According to the Big Bang theory, the universe is finite (limited) in size. Moreover, if the beginning of the current expansion was the beginning of the universe, the universe is also finite in age. This view clashed with the view that the universe had always existed and was infinite in extent.

The chief rival of the Big Bang theory was the "steady-state" theory, which Austrians Herman Bondi and Thomas Gold and Briton Fred Hoyle proposed in 1949. According to the steady-state theory, the universe had no beginning and will have no end, in either space or time. Morcover, viewed on a large scale, all parts of the universe have always looked, and will always look, essentially the same. This means that new galaxies continually form in the spaces that are left when old galaxies move apart. According to this theory, these new galaxies form from hydrogen atoms that have simply appeared, out of nothing, in space.

Critics of the steady-state theory complained that this theory violated the Law of Conservation of Matter. (This is a physical law that states that matter is never created nor destroyed.) The steady-state theory's supporters correctly responded, however, that the problem of where the matter of the universe came from also existed in the Big Bang theory.

Light Spectra

When light rays of the same color are combined, they either reinforce one another, producing a brighter color, or they cancel one another out, producing darkness. This shows that light has the properties of waves. The visible light spectrum, which results from passing sunlight through a prism, occupies just a small portion of a full spectrum of electromagnetic radiation. This radiation consists of high-speed particles or rays that are emitted by an object. The total spectrum ranges from what are called radio waves to gamma rays.

Astronomers typically describe radiation that comes from a particular part of the electromagnetic spectrum by providing its wavelength. The wavelength is the distance between the crests of two adjacent waves. All of these waves are electromagnetic disturbances traveling through space itself. All of them travel through space at a single speed (the speed of light), which is precisely the same for all forms of electromagnetic radiation.

Astronomers use telescopes to concentrate the light from bodies in space. Sometimes astronomers pass the concentrated light through a prism. This disperses the light into a band of various colors, called a spectrum. The different colors appear because light has different wavelengths. Upon closer inspection, one sees that the spectrum is not a continuous distribution of colors (ranging from violet to red) but is actually broken up by many dark lines.

The surfaces of stars emit a continuous spectrum, or range, of light. Vaporized elements in a star's atmosphere absorb narrow regions of this spectrum, producing a pattern of dark spectral lines. This pattern is the sum of the unique absorption patterns of each of the elements in the star's atmosphere. Hence, from these patterns of lines, scientists can learn the precise chemical composition of a star's atmosphere.

Astronomers can use light spectra to determine the red shift of the radiation from a galaxy. They first obtain the spectrum of its radiation. Then they measure the increase in the wavelengths of its dark spectral lines. Some of these red shifts can be very large; a particular spectral line is sometimes shifted completely out of the visible region of the electromagnetic spectrum and into the infrared or even the radio-wave region.

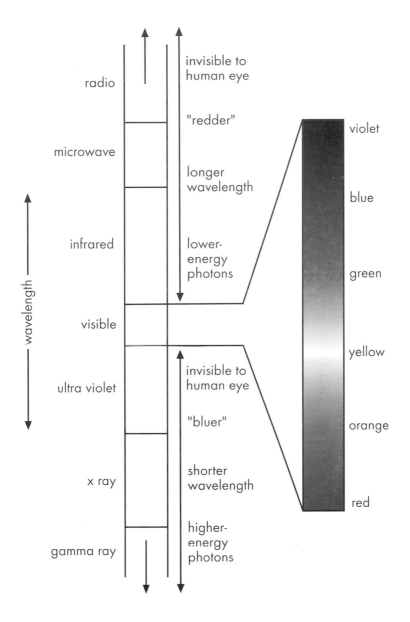

The electromagnetic spectrum ranges from radio waves to gamma rays. The light that is visible to the naked eye makes up a small part of the electromagnetic spectrum.

Tragedy, Love, and Accomplishment

At Cambridge University, Hawking had expected to do his graduate work under Fred Hoyle, then one of the world's most famous astronomers and cosmologists. Hawking was therefore initially disappointed when the university assigned him to work in the research group of another scientist. He was told he had to work with Dennis Sciama, a lesser-known cosmologist.

However, the university's decision proved to be advantageous. Sciama was an expert on Einstein's general theory of relativity. Hawking soon realized that Sciama was an excellent scientist. What is more, unlike Hoyle, who was frequently away on trips presenting his views to other scientists, Sciama was nearly always available to Hawking to provide stimulation and support.

Hawking got off to a rocky start: He quickly realized that he had not learned enough mathematics at Oxford to handle the difficult calculations associated with the general relativity theory. He was also having trouble choosing a research topic that was both interesting and easy enough to complete in graduate school.

But most worrisome was the fact that Hawking's physical condition had significantly worsened. He had never had good coordination, but now he seemed to be getting even clumsier. He fell over several times without any reason, and his hands seemed less useful than they had been before. At first, the Hawkings passed these difficulties off as anxiety about exams. But eventually, Isobel urged him to see a doctor. At this point, however, the doctors did not find anything seriously wrong with him.

Albert Einstein developed the general theory of relativity that provided one of the first ways to theorize about the universe.

Hawking decided to go to Iran with a friend in the summer of 1962. During the journey, however, he became very ill—so ill that he visited a doctor in the Iranian city of Tabriz. When he and his friend returned to England, Stephen was quite worn out.

His odd physical clumsiness continued. When Stephen's parents saw him sometime after his trip, they could tell that he was not in good health. Reasonably enough for a doctor of tropical medicine, his father, Frank, thought that his son's health problem was a result of the illness Stephen had contracted while he was traveling in the Middle East. But that was not the case.

During the following winter, his mother recalled, Hawking fell while ice skating—and he could not get up. It was now clear that something was very wrong. Once again, he went for a medical checkup. This time, however, the news was bad.

In January 1963, shortly after his 21st birthday, doctors told Stephen that he had a progressive disease called amyotrophic lateral sclerosis (ALS, also known as Lou Gehrig's disease). Hawking was told that the disease was incurable and that it was unpredictable. It might stop its progression for a period of time, and it might just arrest (stop its advance entirely)—but it would never get better. The doctors also could not say when the disease would kill him; it could be a matter of just a few months or of many years. Since Hawking had developed the disease at a much younger age than was the norm, the doctors believed that death would occur sooner rather than later. Hawking himself thought that he was likely to die within a few years; and indeed, the doctors told his mother that he probably had no more than two and a half years to live.

The doctors' diagnosis plunged Hawking into a deep depression. He initially shut himself up in his room and listened to tragic operas by the German composer Richard Wagner. During this time, he was also plagued by disturbing nightmares.

The shocking news about his health had one positive result: eventually it changed his entire outlook on life. The world-weariness he felt during his Oxford years now lifted. He now found himself thinking of all the things he would accomplish if he were saved from this disease. He was no longer bored by life but, rather, thought about how he could improve the lives of others. He also came to believe that he was lucky in his choice of theoretical physics as a career, because the nature of the work would allow him to continue his research despite the handicaps associated with ALS.

Hawking's recovery from depression was due in large part to his developing relationship with a young woman named Jane Wilde. He had met her at a New Year's Eve party shortly before doctors had diagnosed his disease. Jane was in her last year in the public high school in St. Albans. Westfield College in London had accepted her as a student, and she planned to study modern languages there beginning in fall 1963. Hawking's brilliance had immediately struck Wilde. She and Hawking soon started seeing each other frequently. Within a short time, they had fallen in love.

Hawking's condition worsened. Walking soon became very difficult for him, but he insisted on moving himself whenever possible, instead of having others help him. He had to grab onto walls and furniture to move about in a room, and he needed a walking stick to cross an open space. His speech became almost impossible for strangers to understand, and his close associates could understand him only

Amyotrophic Lateral Sclerosis

Amyotrophic lateral sclerosis (ALS), which first struck Stephen Hawking as a college student, is a disease that destroys the nerves that carry messages from the brain to the muscles that cause the body's voluntary movements. In the United States, ALS is often called "Lou Gehrig's disease," after the famous New York Yankees first baseman, who died of the illness in the late 1930s.

As Hawking experienced, the first symptom of ALS is minor muscle weakness. Eventually, however, all of the body's voluntary muscles—except for the muscles that control eye movement—become completely paralyzed. Often with this disease, healthy muscles will waste away through disuse.

The disease does not kill its victims directly; those who suffer from it typically die of respiratory failure, caused by pneumonia or other infection. As the disease progresses, the mind and the senses remain unimpaired. Some sufferers have described this condition as "a kind of living death." Stephen Hawking, however, has been able to thrive through the vigorous life of his brain.

Roughly one in every 20,000 people has ALS. Fifty percent of ALS patients die within three years; only ten percent survive beyond ten years. In up to 20 percent of ALS patients, the disease stops progressing for long periods of time—sometimes it even stops permanently.

Until very recently, ALS has been untreatable by doctors. Respirators have helped ALS patients to breathe, however, and some patients who are not able to swallow have been kept alive through the use of feeding tubes.

Recently, medical researchers have learned that ALS is not just one disease. Instead, it is four or more different diseases in which a particular type of chemical malfunction occurs in the motor nerve cells. These recent discoveries have suggested treatments that may slow the progression of some forms of ALS. Some of these treatments have already shown great promise in clinical trials.

Lou Gehrig's baseball career with the New York Yankees lasted for
14 years. When he left the game in 1939, because of the crippling
effects of ALS, he held the record for most consecutive games
played—2,130. ALS was eventually named after him.

The Special Theory of Relativity and Space-Time

Ever since the time of Galileo, scientists have known that the speed of objects is not absolute but makes sense only when measured relative to some point of reference. The building in which we live, for example, appears to us to be standing still. An observer on the Sun, however, would see the building as moving—revolving about the Earth's axis and orbiting the Sun.

Until the first decade of this century, people believed that time and space were two completely separate and independent things. Physicists regarded positions in space and the times at which events occurred as "absolute quantities"; that is, these positions would be the same from the point of view of all observers, no matter what their speed or location.

In 1905, Albert Einstein demolished these common-sense views with his "special theory of relativity." Einstein based this theory on a surprising observation about light: Every observer perceives light as traveling through space at the same speed—a whopping 186,000 miles per second (almost 670 million miles per hour). This is true no matter how fast or in what direction the observer is moving as compared to the light source.

To show the implications of all observers' seeing light travel at the same speed, Einstein provided a "thought experiment" similar to the following: Imagine a train car traveling in the dark at a constant speed along a straight track. Observer A, riding at the precise middle of the train, triggers a flashbulb when directly beside observer B,

with difficulty. By the end of his second year at Cambridge, however, his condition had stabilized. He began to feel that he had a future.

By 1963, Stephen Hawking had already come to the attention of the scientific community. Fred Hoyle had told one of who is on the ground beside the track. From Observer A's perspective, the illumination of the front and back ends of the car occurs at the same instant, because light from the flash travels the same distance and at the same speed to both ends of the car. From Observer B's perspective, however, these two events (the illumination of the front and back ends) do not occur at the same instant. Observer B observes that the light travels a shorter distance to the rear end of the car than to the front end, because the car is moving forward. Therefore, from Observer B's perspective, the illumination of the rear of the car occurs before the illumination of the front of the car. Thus, the time that passes between two events is not absolute but depends on the motion of the observers.

Einstein also proved that a "stationary observer" sees that the time of a moving object slows and that its length decreases along the direction of its motion. From the object's point of view, the observer is moving. The object "sees" that the observer's time slows and that the observer's length decreases. Thus, both time and length (and therefore space) are not absolute quantities; instead, they depend on the motion of their observers.

In 1908 a scientist named Herman Minkowski built on Albert Einstein's work. Minkowski showed mathematically that time and space do not exist separately; rather, they are united in a four-dimensional space-time. We perceive space and time as separate instead of perceiving a single space-time, because our own motions and the motions we normally observe are much slower than the speed of light.

his graduate students, Jaylant Narlikar, to develop the mathematics needed to support one part of Hoyle's steady-state theory. Hawking became so interested in Narlikar's work that he did the math himself. In doing so, he discovered that the latest part of Hoyle's theory was not valid.

Without waiting for Narlikar to complete his assigned work, Hoyle presented his latest findings at a meeting of The Royal Society of London. At the end of the meeting, Hawking publicly reported that his own calculations showed that the theory could not possibly be correct. The embarrassed Hoyle was furious, but he and Hawking soon made up.

Hawking wrote a paper summarizing his mathematical results. This work gave him a reputation among cosmologists as a man to pay attention to.

In 1964, after Hawking had gotten over his depression, he and Jane Wilde became engaged. Hawking now began to take his work very seriously, feeling that if he was to be married, he would have to finish his doctoral degree and get a job. To his surprise, he found that he enjoyed the discipline of working hard. He wrote a Ph.D., or doctoral, thesis (a lengthy paper required to receive a doctoral degree) and passed the final examination in 1965, when he was just 23.

MARRIED LIFE BEGINS

While completing his thesis, Hawking applied for, and received, a research "fellowship" at Gonville and Caius College at Cambridge University. People who were given such fellowship positions had only light teaching responsibilities and spent most of their time conducting research. Although the income from this fellowship was not generous, it was enough to support a family, so Hawking and Jane Wilde were married in July 1965.

After a brief honeymoon in England, Jane and Stephen flew off to spend some time at Cornell University in New

York. As a student in the summer institute program on relativity theory, Stephen met many leading researchers in this field from all over the world.

In the fall of 1965, back in Cambridge, Stephen and Jane found a house that was close enough to the Department of Applied Mathematics and Theoretical Physics for Stephen to be able to walk to work. Jane commuted back and forth between Cambridge and London until she received her college degree in modern languages (in the summer of 1966). Once Jane was living full time at Cambridge, the Hawking home became the center of an active circle of friends.

Stephen's personal, professional, and social life was going well, but his health had taken another turn for the worse. He had to abandon his cane for a pair of crutches, and it now took him a full 15 minutes to drag himself up one flight of stairs to his bedroom. His speech had also become too slurred for most people to understand. In fact, it was so hard to understand that his friend George Ellis had to read Hawking's paper to the scientific audience attending a prestigious meeting on general relativity in Miami, Florida, in December 1965.

LOOKING INTO THE BIG BANG THEORY

While Stephen Hawking was completing his Ph.D. research paper, the Big Bang theory was receiving powerful observational support. In 1965 Bell Laboratory researchers Arno Penzias and Robert Wilson made a significant discovery: Microwave radiation was reaching the Earth uniformly from every direction in the sky, even from parts of space that contained no visible stars. Penzias and Wilson believed that

The General Theory of Relativity

The "General Theory of Relativity," published in 1915, was Albert Einstein's strikingly successful attempt to explain the force of gravity that acts between bodies. This theory had its origin in Einstein's insight that a person falling freely feels weightless.

Today, our most familiar example of weightlessness is the case of astronauts orbiting the Earth in a spacecraft. Before Einstein's theory, scientists would have explained the orbital motion of a spacecraft and its crew as follows: The natural tendency of all objects is to remain at rest or to move in a straight line at a constant speed. Physicists call this tendency inertia. For an object to change its speed and/or direction of motion, a force must act on it. Therefore, the spaceship and its crew orbit the Earth—instead of traveling in a straight line—because of the gravitational force exerted on them by the Earth.

In essence, Einstein changed the definition of a "straight line." A straight line in space-time, he implied, would be whatever path an object follows if it is not "experiencing" any force acting on it. According

they had detected the remnants of the fireball produced by the Big Bang explosion that had created the universe. Most cosmologists soon agreed with that conclusion.

In late fall 1964, the British mathematician Roger Penrose had used topology, a type of mathematics, to prove a startling prediction based on the theory of general relativity: A sufficiently massive dead star should collapse to a single point. This point was called a "space-time singularity." The "singularity" was a location at which space-time ceased to exist, matter was infinitely dense, and the laws of physics ceased to be valid.

Stephen Hawking

to his view, the natural tendency of any body is to travel at what to it is constant speed along a straight path through space-time. Thus, an orbiting spacecraft follows what to it is a straight-line path. Any portion of space-time, however, is curved by any matter it contains. (The greater the included mass, the greater the curvature of the surrounding space-time.) Because the mass of the Earth curves the space-time that the craft is traveling through, it follows curved paths in our familiar three-dimensional space.

The idea of a curved "straight line" may seem nonsensical, but consider what it means to travel straight to the North Pole from some point on the Earth's equator. Here, "straight" means the shortest distance that one can travel on the curved surface of the Earth.

The mathematics associated with Einstein's general theory of relativity is extremely complicated. Usually, finding exact solutions to most of his equations is not even possible. But the great general relativists, like Stephen Hawking, have been good at selecting suitable simplifying assumptions. Such assumptions enable the equations to be solved while still providing results that correspond realistically to the actual physical situation being investigated.

Learning of Penrose's result, Stephen Hawking had suggested a brilliant idea for his thesis topic: Hawking would investigate whether the universe had started as a singularity and had then expanded outward. This idea had immediately gained Sciama's approval. Hawking used this topic for his doctoral thesis.

To complete his thesis quickly, Hawking had made a simplifying assumption to make the mathematics easier: He assumed that the universe is now expanding so fast that it will never collapse. Hawking realized that this assumption was questionable. The universe might in fact contain

The observations of Robert Wilson (left) and Arno Penzias (right) gave significant support to the Big Bang theory.

enough matter for gravity to cause the expansion to slow, stop, and turn into a contraction.

After Hawking had completed his thesis, he collaborated with Penrose to develop the powerful new mathematical techniques necessary to avoid the need for any simplifying assumptions. These efforts were successful. In 1970, Hawking and Penrose published a joint paper that mathematically proved a profound conclusion—that, according to the general theory of relativity, the space, time, and matter/energy that together make up our universe all came into existence suddenly and simultaneously as a "big-bang singularity."

Hawking and Penrose's proof created an intellectual crisis for scientific cosmologists. All scientific laws and theories relate to events that occur in time and in space. Neither time nor space, however, would exist in an initial singularity; they would come into existence only at the Big Bang. Thus, while scientists could say with certainty that the universe had a beginning, they could not say precisely how the universe had begun.

Explorations
Into
Space-Time

The late 1960s brought many exciting changes to Stephen Hawking's life. The Hawkings' first child, Robert, was born in 1967. In 1968, Hawking became a staff member at the Institute of Theoretical Astronomy, where he worked three mornings a week. The Institute was on the outskirts of Cambridge, much farther from his home, so he obtained a three-wheeled car outfitted for disabled drivers to get to work. The Institute did all that it could to accommodate Hawking's physical disabilities. In turn, Hawking's growing reputation soon attracted many promising students to the Institute.

In the meantime, Jane was also working very hard. Because of Stephen's illness, all of the tasks of caring for the family and of running the household fell upon her. She and Stephen tried their best not to focus on his illness, preferring to live life to the fullest while the opportunity still existed; they did, after all, realize that because of his disease, Stephen might die at any time.

But Jane's everyday chores and responsibilities were demanding. Stephen needed special assistance, and he physically could not help with caring for the children and the house. Jane had consciously chosen to channel her energies into her family rather than a career. However, it must have been particularly hard for her to shoulder these many daily responsibilities while Stephen was collecting more awards and praise in the scientific world.

By 1970, the Hawkings had another child, this time a daughter, Lucy. At this point, however, Hawking had to abandon his crutches for a wheelchair. Disillusioned by the medical advice that Stephen was getting, his father, Frank, read up on amyotrophic lateral sclerosis. Frank eventually prescribed vitamin and steroid therapy in the hopes of strengthening his son's deteriorating muscles.

Looking into Black Holes

Hawking's early work in cosmology had displayed his unusual mastery of the difficult mathematics connected with Albert Einstein's general theory of relativity. This theory had been the basis of his and Roger Penrose's unsettling conclusion that the universe had started from a singularity (a point in space-time at which the ordinary laws of physics break down). Their conclusion soon gained wide acceptance by cosmologists, who could find no flaws in their mathematics.

Few, if any, questioned the crucial assumption that the general theory of relativity by itself could account for the large-scale features of the universe. In 1974, however, Hawking demolished this assumption. He discovered that a complete cosmological theory must also incorporate quantum theory—the theory of the very small, as in atoms and subatomic particles. This discovery emerged from an intense theoretical study of black holes—certain regions of space-time—that he undertook beginning in 1970.

One of the most surprising predictions of Albert Einstein's general theory of relativity was that gravity should act not just on ordinary matter; it should also act on electromagnetic radiation. According to Einstein's theory, each ray should follow what is to the ray a straight line through space-time. This would result in its following a spatially curved path, however, when it travels through space-time that matter has curved.

Verification of this 1916 prediction quickly followed. In 1919, a group of scientists led by British physicist Arthur Eddington observed a total eclipse of the Sun. They found that light from stars in line with the Sun was bent by 1.75 seconds of arc (a second is $1/3,600$ of a degree) by the Sun's gravity—exactly the amount predicted by Einstein's theory. Consequently, this theory soon gained acceptance by most of the world's leading theoretical physicists.

The theory suggested that electromagnetic radiation could not escape from a sufficiently curved region of space-time. But that suggestion raised another question: Does the universe contain any concentrations of matter high enough to cause this much curvature? In 1939 physicist J. Robert

Physicist J. Robert Oppenheimer's studies of electromagnetic
radiation helped other physicists understand black holes.

Oppenheimer and his student Hartland Snyder proved that it did, through a theoretical study of stars that were cooling down at the end of their life cycles. Their calculations showed that, as a star cooled, the gravitational attraction between its particles caused it to collapse into a smaller and smaller volume. Once a star with a mass greater than three times that of our Sun had collapsed to a certain volume, its electromagnetic radiation could no longer escape into the surrounding universe. The region of space that had contained the star had thus become what was later to be named a black hole.

Einstein's general theory of relativity also predicted that time is slower where space-time is more highly curved. Scientists verified this prediction in 1976. They used very accurate clocks to compare ground-level time with time in a rocket in the upper atmosphere. As predicted, time passed more slowly at ground level, where the Earth's gravitational force is greater and therefore its space-time curvature is greater. The theory predicted that time stops completely in regions of space-time that are curved enough to trap electromagnetic radiation.

During World War II, and in the early phase of the subsequent Cold War period, when the United States and the Soviet Union were in a race for world supremacy, most of the world's theoretical physicists were busy working on military research for their governments. Oppenheimer, for example, led the American effort that developed the first atomic bomb. It was not until the late 1950s, therefore, that astrophysicists (physicists who study the physical and chemical makeup of celestial objects) paid serious attention to Oppenheimer and Snyder's results. Then, American and Soviet physicists confirmed their conclusions, using the

A Collapsing Star

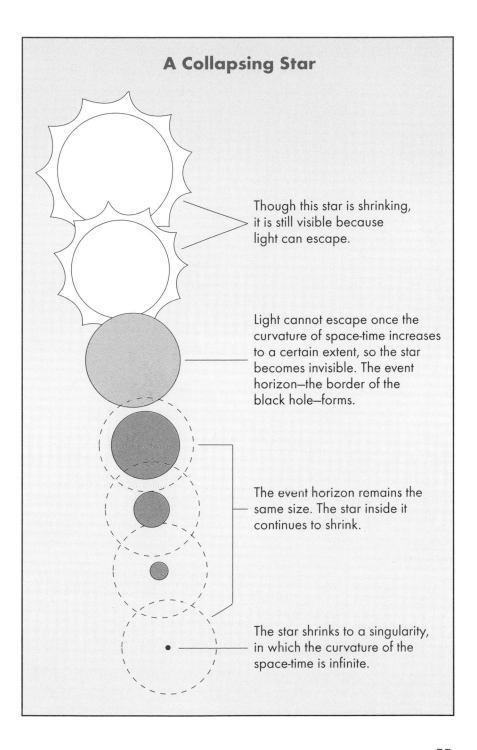

Though this star is shrinking, it is still visible because light can escape.

Light cannot escape once the curvature of space-time increases to a certain extent, so the star becomes invisible. The event horizon—the border of the black hole—forms.

The event horizon remains the same size. The star inside it continues to shrink.

The star shrinks to a singularity, in which the curvature of the space-time is infinite.

much more detailed mathematical models that nuclear weapons experts had used to develop hydrogen bombs.

Although the pace of research in this area then sped up, confusion was the norm. Scientists involved could not agree on what issues associated with the collapse of stars were the most likely to yield clear-cut results.

The major role in focusing this research was the invention of the term *black hole* in 1967 by Princeton University theoretical physicist John Wheeler. A black hole is a region of space-time in which gravity is so strong that neither electromagnetic radiation nor matter can escape from it to the surrounding universe. The boundary of the black hole is called an "event horizon." Within a short time, the term *black hole* had gained acceptance among the scientific community and had helped bring this area of theoretical astronomy to public attention. Black holes soon became the most dreaded objects of the universe in science fiction, permanently swallowing up spacecraft that ventured too near to them.

Once theorists had decided that there probably were such things as black holes, the search was on to discover them in the heavens. Typical black holes would neither emit nor reflect electromagnetic radiation; therefore, astronomers could not detect them directly with typical astronomical telescopes. In addition, typical black holes would be too small or too distant to be observed by their blocking a star from our view or bending its light. The types of gravity-wave detectors that scientists expect will detect black holes directly will not be completed and working until shortly after the year 2000. For these reasons, astronomers recognized that they would have to detect black holes indirectly—from their effect on observable celestial objects. Scientists have since discovered many likely black-hole candidates.

John Wheeler, a theoretical physicist from Princeton
University, invented the term *black hole* in 1967.

"Black Holes Have No Hair"

Starting in the mid-1960s, theoretical physicists tried to figure out the properties of black holes. These attempts involved mathematical analyses based on the general theory of relativity. The big question was this: Are black holes as different from one another and as complicated as the diverse stars and other objects from which they might form, or are they much simpler?

By 1970, the work of Roger Penrose and others had established that the complete collapse of any nonrotating star (most stars are thought to be rotating) would result in the formation of a perfectly round black hole. Stephen Hawking played a major role in solving the extremely difficult mathematical equations that were necessary to extend these conclusions to the far-more-typical case in which the collapsing object was rotating.

By 1973, he and his colleagues had reached the following conclusions, in his words from his book *A Brief History of Time*: "After gravitational collapse a black hole must settle down to a state in which it could be rotating, but not pulsating. Moreover, its size and shape would depend only on its mass and rate of rotation, and not on the nature of the body that had collapsed to form it. This result became known by the maxim: 'A black hole has no hair.'"

This theory was extremely useful to scientists because it put limits on the number of black-hole types. The "no-hair" theory also meant that much information about a body that has collapsed is lost in black-hole formation. This helped to focus research and allowed models of objects that might contain black holes to be made.

Stephen Hawking

A Passionate Personality

Hawking traveled a great deal in the early 1970s, giving talks about the nature of the universe and attending professional meetings all over the world. His fame as a scientist had spread, and his public image was also developing—in ways both positive and negative. Hawking was very popular among the students at the Institute, and women considered him charming—in fact, he has been described as flirtatious during this period. Yet people also found him to be sometimes irritable, impatient, and demanding.

Some of Hawking's unhappiness was due to the fact that his physical disabilities were becoming more limiting. It became even harder for him to speak clearly, and he was having trouble writing out the mathematics required for his work—he was no longer able to use pencil and paper. Instead, he worked out equations in his mind.

His recall and his ability to think things through entirely in his mind became legendary. One secretary at the Institute told the story of how Hawking remembered a minute error that he had made the previous day while dictating 40 pages of equations!

Mini Black Holes and Hawking Radiation

One evening in November 1970, during the difficult process of getting ready for bed, Hawking was examining various space-time images of black holes in his mind. Suddenly he had an insight that had a profound implication: The total surface area of all of the black holes in the universe must

Black Holes and the Second Law of Thermodynamics

In November 1970, Stephen Hawking quickly noted the similarity between his discovery that the total surface area of the universe's black holes must increase with the generally accepted law that the entropy of the universe continually increases.

The entropy of a "system" (a region of space and the matter and energy it contains) is a measure of the randomness in the distribution of its particles and energy. The greater the randomness or disorder, the greater the entropy.

According to the second law of thermodynamics, in a system that can neither lose nor gain matter or energy—called a "closed system"—the entropy always increases to its maximum value. The universe is a closed system, so its entropy always increases.

The entropy of a system always increases for the following reason: Many more random (disorganized) arrangements of its contents than organized arrangements are possible. To understand this idea, think about what happens when you shuffle a new deck of cards. There are only a few ways in which you can group all of the cards in numerical order in separate suits, but there are billions of ways in which you can scramble the cards randomly. This is why you would have to shuffle for a very long time before the deck would accidentally return to the original arrangement.

Increase of entropy plays a major role in almost every change that occurs in nature. It explains, for instance, why a single drop of food

continually increase over time. This view, strikingly similar to the Second Law of Thermodynamics, led, over the next four years, to his most famous discovery: what would become known as "Hawking radiation."

Any amount of matter can, in theory, become a black hole if it is sufficiently compressed. In 1971, Hawking speculated coloring eventually becomes completely mixed with the water it is added to—but never separates out again. It also explains why heat moves from a hot object to an adjacent cold object, until both have the same temperature.

In many processes, such as the freezing of water, entropy appears to decrease. But the decrease in entropy in one location is more than offset by an accompanying increase in entropy in other locations. In the case of the freezing of water, the water loses entropy as its loss of heat causes its particles to take fixed positions in a crystal lattice, a geometric arrangement showing the positions of atoms, molecules, or ions in a crystal. The heat lost from the water raises the temperature of the surrounding air, however, increasing its entropy. The entropy gained by the air is greater than the entropy lost by the water. As a result, entropy increases overall in the freezing process.

Hawking initially thought that black holes were too simple to have entropy. Princeton University graduate student Jacob Bekenstein dis-agreed. Bekenstein's position appeared extremely weak when Hawking pointed out that if black holes had entropy, they would have temperature and hence would emit electromagnetic radiation into the extremely cold (absolute zero temperature) space surround-ing them. This was a possibility that even Bekenstein rejected as being inconsistent with the very idea of black holes. In 1974, however, Bekenstein's belief that black holes had entropy was proven correct—when Hawking reported his brilliant theoretical discovery of what is now called "Hawking radiation."

that "mini" black holes might have formed shortly after the Big Bang, which he, along with many others, believed had created the universe.

The dimensions of these mini black holes would be very small—smaller than the size of an atom. Hawking began to develop the complex mathematics to support this theory

QUANTUM MECHANICS

In the 1890s, a crisis arose in physics: Physicists discovered that the spectral distribution of light—that is, its intensity throughout its range of wavelengths—emitted from any body at a particular temperature did not agree with the theoretical prediction of its distribution. In 1900, German physicist Max Planck reported that the theory and the experiment agreed if he made the following assumption: Any body emitting electromagnetic radiation—thus, any body—could not have any arbitrary amount of energy. Instead, it could have only amounts of energy that were whole-number multiples of an extremely small, but finite, amount of energy. Planck called this least-possible quantity of energy a "quantum" (plural "quanta") of energy.

In 1905, Albert Einstein used Planck's idea that energy occurred as quanta to explain how ultraviolet light dislodged electrons from certain metals when it struck them. Einstein showed that light, and every other form of electromagnetic radiation, did not behave solely as a wave. A ray of electromagnetic radiation also had the nature of a particle, which soon got the name "photon." Einstein showed that each photon corresponding to a particular wavelength of light had an energy equal to Planck's quanta multiplied by the speed of light and divided by the wavelength.

and to defend his observations about the properties of black holes. Because of the extremely small size of these black holes, Hawking had to use principles of quantum mechanics. He was a pioneer in joining these principles with general relativity theory, a joining that eventually led to his greatest scientific contribution.

In September 1973, Hawking traveled to Moscow, the capital of the then–Soviet Union and the republic of Russia,

Stephen Hawking

The French physicist Louis de Broglie speculated in 1924 that if electromagnetic radiation had a dual wave/particle nature, the same would be the case for ordinary matter. He used Einstein's energy/wavelength relationship to predict the wavelength that would correspond to electrons with a particular energy. In 1927, the demonstration of electron diffraction when a beam of electrons struck a crystal showed that electrons were both waves and particles, as de Broglie had predicted.

If electrons were waves, it made no sense to imagine a precise location for them at each instant of time; the same was true for other particles the size of atoms or smaller. Werner Heisenberg, a German physicist, formalized this notion in 1924, in his famous "uncertainty principle." According to Heisenberg, the greater the certainty in the position of an object, the greater the uncertainty in its speed (and therefore in its energy), and vice versa. The uncertainty is not large enough to affect our experience of objects large enough for us to see with our eyes, but it is significant at the atomic scale.

The discovery that electrons have a dual wave/particle nature was the starting point for the development of modern quantum mechanics. Quantum mechanics explains the physical and chemical properties of all of the chemical elements. Scientists have also used quantum theory with great success to explain the behavior of subatomic particles.

where he discussed black holes with black-hole experts Yakov Zel'dovich and Alexander Starobinsky. They argued that, according to a theory called the "uncertainty principle," developed by Werner Heisenberg, rotating black holes should create and radiate, or emit, particles. (According to the uncertainty principle, there is no such thing as completely empty space—that is, space that contains neither matter nor energy.) This radiation of particles would cause

Explorations into Space-Time

Werner Heisenberg developed the uncertainty principle, which
was used by Hawking in his explanation of black-hole radiation.

Stephen Hawking

EQUIVALENCE OF MASS AND ENERGY

One of the most important consequences of Einstein's special theory of relativity is that matter can change into an equivalent quantity of energy, and vice versa. Einstein represented this equivalence with his famous equation $E = mc^2$, where E is energy, m is mass (the quantity of matter), and c is the speed of light in a vacuum.

Because c is so huge (186,000 miles per second), a small amount of mass is equivalent to a large amount of energy. The conversion of matter to energy is the basis for nuclear weapons and nuclear power. It is also the source of the tremendous quantities of energy that are released by the Sun and other stars—hydrogen nuclei join to produce helium nuclei, and a small fraction of the total mass of the hydrogen nuclei changes into a huge amount of energy in the process. The conversion of energy to matter is crucial to many of cosmology's most important theories.

Today, scientists can convert energy to matter in high-energy particle accelerators, and current theories hold that the Big Bang resulted in conversion of a large amount of energy in the universe into matter.

the black holes to lose energy, and this loss would slow their rotation rate. Once they stopped rotating, they no longer would emit radiation.

Hawking was impressed by their theory, but not with the mathematics that they had used to come to these conclusions. He therefore set out to find a better approach.

He revealed his mathematic approach at a meeting in Oxford, England, in November 1973. He supported the idea that black holes had radiation. However, he had not yet done the calculations to show just how *much* radiation would be emitted.

GETTING HOTTER WHILE LOSING ENERGY

It is our familiar experience that objects get cooler, not hotter, as they lose energy. At night, for example, the surface of the Earth cools as it radiates heat energy (as infrared radiation) into outer space.

Black holes and other systems in which the various parts interact with each other mainly through the force of gravity, however, behave differently. They typically get hotter as they lose gravitational energy—as their parts are pulled closer and closer together.

An example is the formation of stars from massive clouds of dust. The gravitational attraction between the dust particles in a cloud causes them to accelerate toward one another. This causes the cloud to shrink. Simultaneously, its temperature increases, because its particles are moving faster. The cloud eventually becomes so hot and so dense that it begins to produce energy through the fusion of atomic nuclei in its center. At that instant, a star is born. The heat produced by the nuclear reaction keeps the star from shrinking further. In fact, it will grow until all of its nuclear fuel is used up.

When Hawking did complete the mathematical calculations, he found that nonrotating black holes would create and emit particles at a steady rate. At first, Hawking was worried that this surprising finding was the result of a mistake on his part. But he soon came to have faith that his calculations were valid and that the steady emission of particles really existed.

Hawking's explanation of black-hole radiation, which became known as "Hawking radiation," depends heavily on the uncertainty principle. The radiation causes a black hole to lose energy and therefore an equivalent quantity of mass. As the black hole loses mass/energy through this

Hawking Radiation

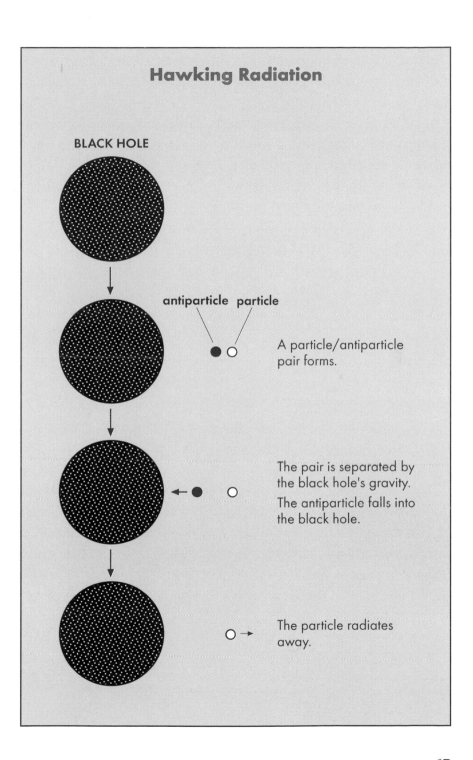

BLACK HOLE

antiparticle   particle

A particle/antiparticle pair forms.

The pair is separated by the black hole's gravity.

The antiparticle falls into the black hole.

The particle radiates away.

Hawking radiation, it shrinks and gets hotter. It gets so hot—trillions of degrees—that it explodes and vanishes completely.

Hawking's calculations showed that large black holes, like the ones that would form by the gravitational collapse of dying stars, would not evaporate in this manner. They were much too big and thus had much too low a temperature. Instead, they would get bigger and bigger, and cooler and cooler, by capturing matter and energy from the outside.

Hawking first announced his results at a conference in February 1974, and they were first published in the following month. At first, black-hole experts thought that Hawking had made a terrible mistake. Perhaps his theoretical foundations were faulty or he had made a mathematical miscalculation, they suggested. During the next several years, however, one by one, these experts all decided that Hawking was correct. Zel'dovich and Starobinsky held out until September 1975. They then discovered that in applying their theory, which was equivalent to Hawking's, they had made a calculation error.

In March 1974, shortly after he had reported his surprising discovery, Hawking was elected to be a fellow (member) of Britain's old and highly prestigious Royal Society. At age 32, Hawking was one of the youngest scientists ever elected to the Society.

Toward a "Theory of Everything"

By the mid-1970s, Stephen Hawking could no longer feed himself or get himself out of bed. Now only his family and closest associates could understand his speech. But while Hawking was not able to express himself well verbally, he became very adept at maneuvering with his wheelchair. To express his annoyance or frustration with people, for example, he would sometimes drive over their toes with his wheelchair. He often displayed a certain recklessness with the vehicle. On the other hand, his maneuvering skill provided a way for Hawking to play with his children.

To cope with the physical demands of his disabilities, the Hawkings now started having one of Stephen's students live in the house with them. In return for helping with Stephen's care and with household chores, a student would receive free room and board—plus a unique opportunity to get to know Hawking and his thinking.

The university provided the Hawkings with a large ground-floor apartment, spacious enough to accommodate the growing family. The apartment was by a large yard in which the children could play. The apartment's wide doorways made it easy for Hawking to ride from room to room, and because it was on one floor, he no longer had to drag himself upstairs to get to his bedroom.

He could no longer drive the three-wheel car that he had used since the late 1960s, but riding to work in his wheelchair—a short ten-minute drive—gave him greater freedom. He did not have to depend on people to carry him from his car to his office.

In 1976, Hawking came to the attention of the general British public when he was featured in the BBC television program "The Key to the Universe." The program featured both his attempt to unite relativity theory with quantum mechanics and his life as a person with severe physical disabilities. A year later, perhaps in response to his growing professional and public fame, Cambridge University gave him a specially created position called "Chair of Gravitational Physics," a lifetime appointment. Two years later, the university appointed Hawking the Lucasian Professor of Mathematics, a position and title that the great Isaac Newton had once held. Hawking's signature in the register book for this position was the last time that he ever signed his name.

Stephen was gaining professional and public acclaim, but Jane was feeling increasingly frustrated in her role of nurse and mother. To regain her sense of self-pride in an environment that prized intellectual accomplishment above all else, she earned an advanced degree in medieval languages, studying Spanish and Portuguese poetry. She then got a position teaching languages in a Cambridge high school. On top of all this, she and Stephen had their third child, Timothy, in 1979.

RETURN TO COSMOLOGY

Until 1974, Hawking had provided extremely precise mathematical proof for any conclusions that he drew about the origin of the universe or about black holes. Starting in 1974, however, his work became more speculative. Rather than get bogged down with mathematical details, he now attempted to discover a basic approach to unify general relativity theory and quantum theory into a "theory of quantum gravity." He hoped that such a theory, when developed by himself and others, would help to explain the origin of the universe.

In the 1970s, Hawking and others pointed out an important observation about the universe. If its earliest conditions had been even slightly different, it would never have developed in a way that would make possible the eventual appearance of human life. Is human existence, then, just a fortunate coincidence, or did a creator specifically design the universe with initial conditions and physical laws such that humans would eventually appear through evolution? Are there many universes with different properties? Do we just

ISAAC NEWTON (1642-1727)

Isaac Newton was unquestionably one of the greatest scientists of all time. He is perhaps most famous for his three laws of motion and his theory of universal gravitation. Newton used these laws to account for the motions of the moon and the planets, as well as the motions of objects on the Earth's surface. Newton's laws apply to the vast majority of cases dealt with by today's scientists and engineers. They fail only in the cases of bodies moving almost at the speed of light or close to a massive object such as the Sun. In those cases, scientists must use Albert Einstein's more general theory of gravitation.

Newton was the first to discover that white light is a mixture of different spectral colors. He used this discovery to explain the apparent color of bodies: Their colors depend on what portions of the visible spectrum they absorb and what portions they reflect or transmit. He was the first to suggest that light rays consist of tiny, rapidly moving particles. Guided by his discoveries concerning light, Newton constructed the first telescope that used a concave mirror (having a deep center and curving upward toward the outer edges) to concentrate light from the faint object being viewed. This design is the basis for today's most powerful telescopes.

Newton was a coinventor (along with German philosopher Gottfried Wilhelm Leibniz) of calculus, the basic mathematical tool used even today by physical scientists. His development of the modern idea of matter and mass was crucial to the development of the modern science of chemistry.

Newton's accomplishments were so significant that he became a popular figure even in his own day. His brilliant use of reason encouraged people to apply reason to all areas of life—including politics and religion—that previously had been governed strictly by tradition. The consequences of this influence were literally revolutionary, leading ultimately to the replacement of absolute monarchies (where authority of the government resides in the hereditary ruler) by democracies.

Isaac Newton's laws are still basic to science and
engineering, even 270 years after his death.

happen to live in one of the few universes in which initial conditions were such that we could eventually arise through the process of evolution?

In his popular writings, Hawking has sometimes used the "weak anthropic principle." (*Anthropic* means relating to human beings and their existence on Earth.) According to this principle, any theories about our universe and its origin must be consistent with the universe now containing intelligent life. Like most other scientists, Hawking has been very skeptical about the "strong anthropic principle," which states that the very existence of our universe depended on its eventually containing human beings to observe and understand it.

For his inaugural address as Lucasian Professor of Mathematics, on April 29, 1980, Hawking wrote a thought-provoking essay entitled "Is the End in Sight for Theoretical Physics?" One of his students read this essay to the audience, since Hawking's ability to speak had become so diminished. In the essay, Hawking stated that a "unifying theory" was needed to properly explain the universe. What he was looking for was both a scientifically elegant and compelling theory that would answer the following question in physical terms: Why did the universe have the correct initial physical conditions and the correct laws to evolve to the universe we have today?

Hawking noted the progress made by particle physicists. They had discovered a set of laws to explain both "electromagnetic interactions" (as between light and matter) and "weak interactions" (responsible for radioactivity). They had also made significant progress toward the discovery of a "grand unified theory" (GUT). Such a theory would unite the two types of interactions with "strong interactions." (Strong

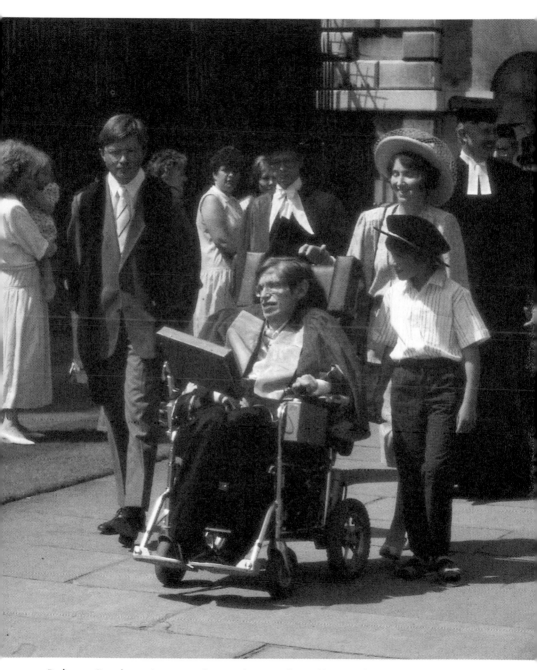

Robert, Stephen, Jane, and Timothy Hawking (from left to right) take part in a procession at Robert's graduation.

Toward a "Theory of Everything"

interactions hold protons and neutrons together in atomic nuclei, and hold quarks together in protons and neutrons.)

Hawking pointed out, though, that theorists had made little, if any, progress toward uniting these three types of interactions with gravity. Much of Stephen Hawking's scientific work since the late 1970s has been directed toward developing a theory of quantum gravity. Such a theory will enable gravity to be incorporated into what he calls a "theory of everything."

Hawking found the key to the development of such a theory when he heard the "sum-over-histories" approach to quantum theory. Richard Feynman, a famous California Institute of Technology (Caltech) theoretical physicist, had developed this approach to explain the paths followed by subatomic particles. Paths that Feynman determined using this technique included those followed by electrons about atomic nuclei and those followed by light rays passing through narrow slits. Hawking learned of Feynman's approach when he spent the 1974–1975 academic year at Caltech in Pasadena, California. Invited there as a Fairchild Distinguished Scholar, Hawking worked on cosmology with his friend Kip Thorne. Jane and the children also spent the year with Stephen in California.

While at Caltech, Hawking had the clever idea of using Feynman's approach to compare the probabilities of different possible histories of the entire universe. To carry out the complicated mathematics involved, Hawking had to use two different kinds of time. Besides "real time"—the time we are all familiar with—he had to use the idea of "imaginary time." This does not mean the same as "make-believe time." Rather, it is time that is represented mathematically by using "imaginary numbers."

Richard Feynman's approach to quantum theory was used by Hawking to explore different possibilities for the history of the universe.

FEYNMAN'S TECHNIQUE

To estimate the probability that any particle starting at any point A could reach any point B, Richard Feynman considered that the particle could follow every possible route, however roundabout. The trip that the particle would have made along each of these routes corresponded to one of its vast number of possible "histories." Feynman made an educated guess that the particle traveled at a constant speed, as a wave, so the wavelength and speed were the same in each of these histories. He then added all these histories. For most of the possible locations of point B, the arriving waves would have canceled one another out; this would mean that the particle had no chance of reaching this location. However, when B was at a few of the many possible locations, the waves would reinforce one another: This would mean that the particle was very likely to reach this location. Paths that Feynman determined using this technique included those followed by electrons about atomic nuclei and those followed by light rays passing through narrow slits.

Imaginary numbers are taught in high school algebra. When any two imaginary numbers are multiplied together, their product is always a negative number. Mathematicians and scientists commonly use imaginary numbers for calculations, especially in quantum mechanics. Using imaginary time enabled Hawking to represent the universe simply as a space-time that had four equivalent dimensions. Scientists call this mathematically simplified space-time "Euclidean space-time," after Euclid, the famous ancient Greek geometer (a specialist in geometry).

In 1981, the Pontifical Academy of Sciences sponsored a conference on cosmology at the Vatican, the seat of the

Roman Catholic Church and a separate country within the city of Rome, Italy. Hawking was one of the cosmologists invited to present a paper during the meeting. Pope John Paul II, the head of the Church, addressed the cosmologists at the end of the conference. Hawking later reported that the pope said to the scientists that it was acceptable to study the evolution of the universe after the Big Bang—but not to study the Big Bang itself. Such an inquiry would challenge Roman Catholic belief that there has been a moment of creation—and hence a creator.

However, in his extremely technical paper presented only a few days earlier, Hawking had done just that—he had challenged Church doctrine, when he suggested that, together, time and space formed a four-dimensional surface. This multi-layered surface was finite in size. However, it did not have any edge or boundary. This would mean that the universe had no beginning.

As Hawking pointed out, viewing the universe as having no beginning created a serious religious dilemma. For, if there was no beginning, there was also no creator.

Hawking spent the following summer in the United States at the University of California at Santa Barbara, working with Jim Hartle, a professor of physics there. The two scientists explored the significance for the universe if space-time had no boundaries. Their results suggested that, as time passes, the universe expands until it reaches a certain maximum size. Then the universe contracts until it occupies a single point—called the "big crunch." Scientists could use their findings to relate the conditions at the Big Bang to how the universe has developed since then; they could also relate the conditions at the big crunch to the preceding state of the universe.

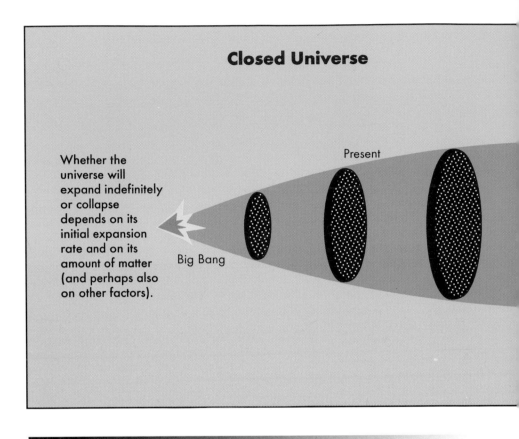

Closed Universe

Whether the universe will expand indefinitely or collapse depends on its initial expansion rate and on its amount of matter (and perhaps also on other factors).

Big Bang

Present

NEAR-DISASTER AND RECOVERY

In the early 1980s, Hawking's physical condition again stabilized. He continued to work intensively, and he traveled around the world giving scientific lectures more frequently than ever. His papers would be read by colleagues, after having been painfully dictated to, and written down by, those few people who could still understand what Hawking was saying.

His popular fame was also growing. In the United States, for example, he was featured in articles in *The New York Times*, *Newsweek*, and *Vanity Fair*.

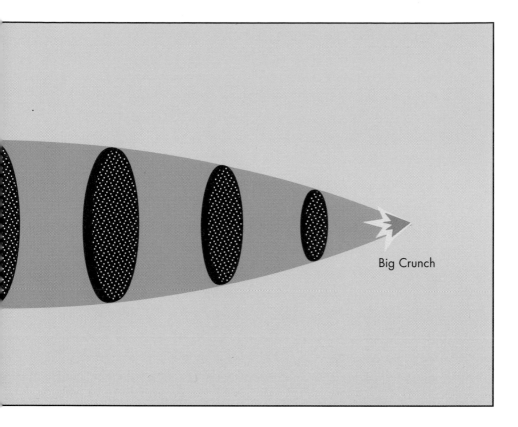

Big Crunch

Jane, in the meantime, was busy looking after her growing family and teaching high school. Consequently, she no longer could accompany Stephen on most of his trips. While traveling, he was now cared for by his research assistants, colleagues, and hired nurses.

Instead of having one of Stephen's students living in the house, the Hawkings now hired nurses to work for a few hours in the morning and evening. The cost of this care was paid for in part by prize money that Stephen had won and by his increased salary, but it still put a great strain on the family budget. In addition, the Hawkings would soon be paying college tuition for their oldest son, Robert, and high school tuition for their daughter, Lucy. Finally, they desperately

Toward a "Theory of Everything"

needed to build up some savings. Inevitably, Stephen's condition would worsen to the point at which he could no longer earn an income to help support the family, and he would require greatly increased nursing care.

These financial concerns played a great part in Hawking's decision, in late 1982, to write a popular book on cosmology. But he had an even more important reason for wanting to write the book: He wanted to reveal to a wide audience the great progress that scientists had made toward "a complete understanding of the laws that govern the universe." Cambridge University Press, which had already published several technical books written or edited by Hawking, offered him a £10,000 advance (then about $17,000) for the rights to the book. Hawking decided, however, that he would rather go with a publisher with extensive experience at marketing books aimed at a mass audience. In the early part of 1984, he signed a contract with the American publishing company Bantam Books. Bantam paid him a guaranteed advance of $250,000 and agreed to pay him a generous part, or royalty, of the purchase price of each book sold. Bantam originally scheduled the book for publication in 1986.

Knowing that Hawking wished to write a best-seller, his editor at Bantam, Peter Guzzardi, worked closely with him to help make his book understandable to a mass audience. Whenever Guzzardi, who had no scientific background, could not understand a passage, he had Hawking rewrite it. By the end of 1984, Hawking had completed a first draft of the book and was working with Guzzardi on all of the necessary changes.

In August 1985, near-disaster struck. While doing research at the European particle physics research institution, CERN, near Geneva, Switzerland, Hawking was rushed to the hospital when he developed breathing difficulties. The doctors discovered that he had an obstruction in his windpipe and feared that he might have pneumonia, which is often fatal to people suffering from ALS. The hospital put him on life support while they attempted to find Jane, who was traveling in Germany.

When Jane arrived at the hospital, the doctors told her that Stephen would be unlikely to survive unless he had a tracheostomy. In this type of operation, a surgeon makes a hole through the neck so air can enter the windpipe below the obstruction. Jane made the difficult decision for Stephen to have the operation, although she thought that this meant that he might never speak again as his speech was barely understandable already. Given that he could not write or type, how would he communicate?

To raise the money for the round-the-clock nursing care that Stephen needed after he returned to England, Jane wrote letters to charitable organizations in many countries. One American foundation agreed to donate the equivalent of about $70,000 per year, and others pledged to help out with smaller contributions.

After this setback, at first Hawking could only communicate by directing his glance at a transparent piece of plastic containing the letters of the alphabet. The person holding the device would watch Hawking's eyes and then guess what letter Hawking was looking at. Whenever the person identified the correct letter, Hawking would raise his eyebrows. Hawking could not hope to continue as a scientist by communicating in this incredibly slow fashion.

Fortunately, because of his celebrity, a California computer expert, Walt Woltosz, heard of his plight. He sent Hawking a copy of a computer program called Equalizer, which he had written for his mother-in-law, who had the same debilitating condition as Hawking. This program causes lines of words—more than 2,500 words in all—to scroll on the computer monitor screen. When the word Hawking wants is in the highlighted line, he presses a switch with his finger. Then, when the desired word in that line is highlighted, he clicks the switch again. When he wants to use a word that is not in the program's vocabulary, he spells the word out by clicking when the desired letter is highlighted.

With this program, Hawking can now use the computer to produce more than 15 words per minute. He also has a formatting program that changes a mathematical equation that he has expressed in words into the corresponding mathematical symbols.

When Hawking has written and edited exactly what he wants to say, he can print it out or, even more important, send it to a voice synthesizer. Hawking is quite pleased with the quality of the speech that is produced by the synthesizer, which sounds nasal but not too robotic. The synthesizer was programmed in California and has what Hawking describes as an American accent, although no American would ever describe the synthesized voice that is produced that way. Thanks to Equalizer and the voice synthesizer, people can now understand Hawking's speech.

David Mason, a Cambridge University computer engineer and friend of Hawking's, created a portable version of the voice synthesizer that was small enough to fit on Stephen's wheelchair. Hawking was then able to lecture to audiences by plugging the synthesizer into a public address system. He could even provide short answers to questions from the audience.

FAME AND FORTUNE

Under the intriguing title *A Brief History of Time*, Hawking's book was published in April 1988. The book is less than 200 pages long and contains only a single equation. Yet the book provides a remarkably complete and careful account, often from a historical point of view, of today's scientific views on the nature and history of the universe.

Jane and Stephen Hawking answer reporters' questions during a 1989 book tour for *A Brief History in Time*.

Because of his speech difficulties, Hawking trained himself to think in an extremely clear and concise manner. *A Brief History of Time* is far from easy to read, but in it, Hawking speaks to readers who lack a scientific background. He often uses striking analogies or clear drawings to illustrate difficult ideas. Some scientists have complained that the book does not make it clear enough that some ideas presented are Hawking's speculations rather than generally accepted "scientific truth." However, this speculative nature of the book makes it valuable as an intellectual biography of Hawking—including his somewhat reckless nature.

Right from the start, *A Brief History of Time* was phenomenally successful. The reviews were excellent, and the book rapidly rose to the top of the nonfiction best-seller charts, where it stayed for months. It remained on *The New York Times* best-seller list for 53 weeks. During 1988, more than half a million copies were sold in the United States alone. The book has been translated into more than 30 languages and has sold more than 8 million copies worldwide. By 1989, income from the sales was pouring in so fast that Hawking no longer needed charitable support for his nursing care, which he still requires around the clock.

By now one of the world's best-known living scientists, Hawking had become a genuine celebrity. The ABC television series "20/20" profiled him, and he was the subject of a BBC documentary entitled "Master of the Universe." With Steven Spielberg—producer and director of the movies *E.T.* and *Close Encounters of a Third Kind*—providing assistance in securing funding, a film version of *A Brief History of Time* was produced. The film is partly a biography of Hawking and partly a visual treatment of some of the scientific ideas that are discussed in his book. It also discusses the

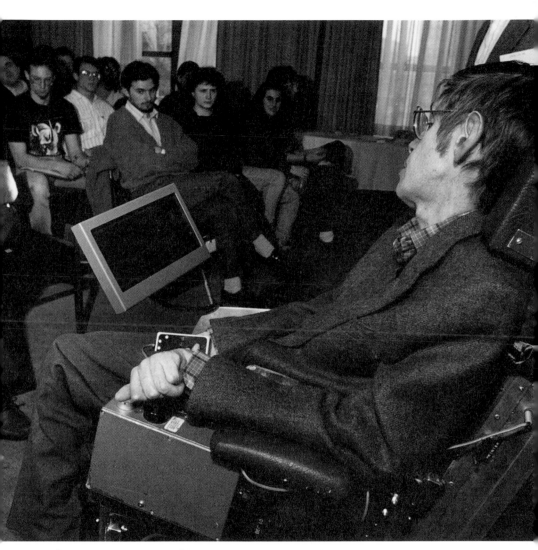

After the publication of his popular book, Hawking
became a much-sought-after lecturer. Here, he talks to
students at Northeastern University, in Boston, in 1990.

religious implications of scientific cosmology and of
Hawking's views in particular. The film opened in late
1991, receiving excellent reviews; in 1992, the film came out
on video cassette. There is now a CD-ROM version as well.

Just as Hawking was reaching the height of fame, however, his marriage fell apart. In the summer of 1990, he and Jane separated after nearly 25 years of marriage. The final break came when Stephen moved into an apartment to live with Elaine Mason, the wife of David Mason, who had created the portable variety of Hawking's speech synthesizer. As Hawking's personal nurse for the previous few years, Elaine had accompanied him constantly when he was at work or traveling around the world, and they had grown quite close.

During the same period, Stephen and Jane had been drifting apart. Stephen had worked and traveled while Jane had pursued her own career and raised the children. What is more, Jane, who had always held strong religious views, had come increasingly to resent Stephen's apparent attempt to reduce the role that God might play in the creation of the universe. Hawking's no-boundary model of the universe particularly upset her. This model reduced, perhaps even eliminated, any role for a creator. Jane felt that her faith had given her the strength and courage to care for Stephen and the children, especially during the financially difficult early years. Stephen's publicly skeptical views were just too hard for her to take.

Eventually, Jane and Stephen divorced. Stephen married Elaine in September 1995 in Cambridge, England.

"WORMHOLES" AND MULTIPLE UNIVERSES

Beginning in the early 1980s, cosmologists began to rival science-fiction writers in the boldness of their speculations. Several prominent cosmologists proposed that the same

Hawking and his new bride, Elaine Mason,
pose on their wedding day in 1995.

process that led to the formation of our universe may have occurred often to form many separate universes.

Some cosmologists have speculated that structures called "wormholes" may actually connect our universe to one or more of these other universes. Some have speculated that short wormholes may connect parts of our own universe that are millions of light-years apart, and that future technology might enable us to use spaceships to travel vast distances through space in an instant, by traveling through a wormhole. Cosmologists have even suggested that people of the future may use wormholes to travel forward and backward in time.

In the late 1980s, Hawking's own work suggested that the singularity in black holes could "give birth" to what he called a "baby universe." This baby universe might connect to a singularity in a black hole a vast distance from the first one. According to the theoretical work performed by Hawking and others, however, it is extremely unlikely that humans could ever travel safely through wormholes or baby universes; it is still more unlikely that wormholes could act as time machines.

Why? In the first place, the entrance to a wormhole is a singularity. If an object of the strongest-known material drew near enough to a singularity, the enormous gravitational force of the singularity would pull it completely apart. This is because the gravitational force of a singularity decreases extremely rapidly with distance. As a result, the singularity pulls much more strongly on the parts of an object right next to it than on parts of the object that are a tiny bit farther away. When gravity acts to separate parts, we call it "tidal gravity," after the manner in which the moon's gravity causes tides in the Earth's oceans.

Stephen Hawking

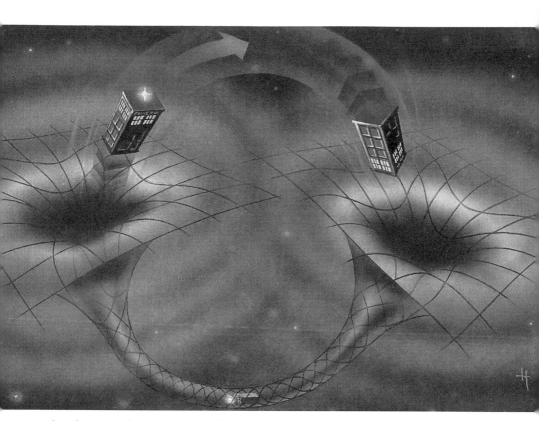

This drawing shows one artist's imaginary journey through space-time within a wormhole.

In the second place, wormholes or singularities are much too narrow for a human to travel through. In fact, they are much narrower than the smallest subatomic particle.

Perhaps in the future, some advanced civilization might invent some material so strong that the tidal gravity of a singularity could not pull it apart. In theory, we could use this material to widen and prop open wormholes; then, perhaps, a robot made of the same remarkable material could travel through the wormhole. Such a material would have properties incredibly different from those of any known material. Well-established chemical theory suggests that we could

Toward a "Theory of Everything"

Hawking uses his voice synthesizer to talk to an audience about black holes and baby universes.

Stephen Hawking

never make such a material using ordinary matter. But even if we could make such a material, that would not end the problem, because bodies similar to those of today's humans could never survive such a trip, even encased in this futuristic material. Tidal gravity would pull them completely apart when they got close enough to the singularity at the entrance to the wormhole.

The odds against a wormhole acting as a time machine are even longer, according to Hawking's "chronology protection conjecture." In it, Hawking argues that whenever someone attempted to use a wormhole for time travel, a strong "vacuum fluctuational beam" would travel through the wormhole, destroying it. In Kip Thorne's book, *Black Holes and Time Warps*, Hawking's friend and colleague quotes him as saying that his conjecture will "keep the world safe for historians."

No
Regrets

On December 25, 1992, the BBC radio program "Desert Island Discs" featured Stephen Hawking as its guest. On the program, Hawking played eight records that he would choose to bring with him to a desert island. His final choice was a record of Edith Piaf singing "Je Ne Regrette Rien" ("I Have No Regrets"), a phrase that he says sums up his life.

If he had his life to live over, Hawking presumably would rather not have ALS. But the richness of his personal and family life, his scientific successes, and the professional and public acclaim he has earned could very well explain his lack of regrets.

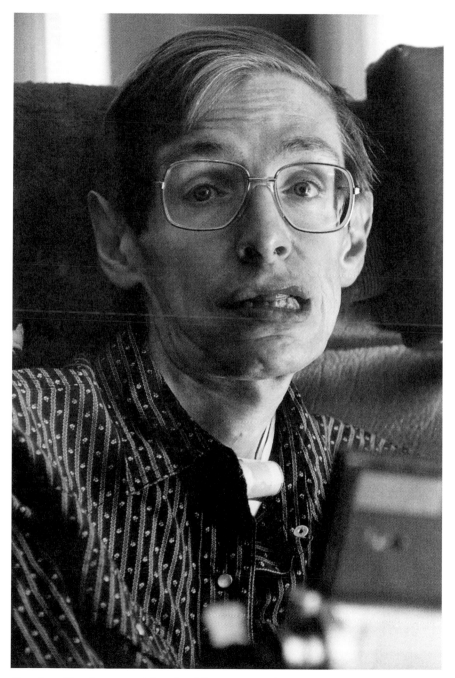

Stephen Hawking says that his life is one without regrets.

In some ways, it is too soon to assess Hawking's historical importance as a scientist. In the first place, his scientific career continues, and his greatest discoveries may still lie ahead. Second, most of his theories deal with phenomena that are difficult or even impossible to observe using current technology. It might be a hundred years or more before scientists can compare the predictions of his theories with observation.

Hawking's scientific peers have nevertheless given him virtually every award available to a theoretical scientist. Moreover, the term "Hawking radiation" has become established in the language of science, ensuring Stephen Hawking at least some degree of scientific immortality.

Among his colleagues, Hawking is most famous for his work on black holes and space-time singularities. During what Kip Thorne calls the "golden age of black-hole research" (1964–1975), Hawking played a major role in establishing that black holes are extremely simple. With Jacob Bekenstein, he showed how to reconcile this simplicity with the fundamental law that the entropy of the universe always increases, by showing that black holes have entropy. His most famous discovery was that black holes are not always "black." For a physicist, an object is "black" if it is not emitting or reflecting radiation in any of the electromagnetic spectrum. But some black holes can emit what has become known as Hawking radiation. Mini black holes can even evaporate and ultimately explode through this process. Hawking radiation is the first prediction resulting from combining general relativity and quantum theory that can be confirmed or rejected by observation.

Hawking also showed that the general theory of relativity alone cannot explain the large-scale structure of today's universe. He showed instead that cosmologists need to use quantum theory to explain the initial conditions of the universe. In his treatment of evaporating black holes, Hawking united these two theories only partially. He treated the black hole itself using the general theory of relativity, and he used quantum mechanics to treat the radiation emitted by the hole. His peers have judged his approach toward merging these two theories as the most successful of the various approaches attempted.

Time will tell if Hawking will be equally successful in creating a quantum theory of space-time itself. However, he has already played a major role in stimulating the search for such a theory.

Scientists in the field of cosmology have grumbled that Stephen Hawking's struggle with ALS has caused his particular scientific views and achievements to obtain more than their fair share of public attention. As compared to the attention that other cosmological theory has received, this may be true. Hawking, however, has used the public's interest in him in a way that is highly beneficial to science overall and to cosmology in particular.

Like every science, cosmology will die out if scientists fail to test its theories experimentally. Much of the testing of cosmological theories involves hugely expensive land-based or space-based telescopes, other instruments, or equally expensive high-energy particle accelerators. The 40-year-long Cold War stimulated an intensive scientific competition between the former Soviet Union and the United States and its Western allies. This resulted in both sides spending a large amount of public money on basic research, much of it in space science and particle physics. With the end of the Cold War, however, public spending on these and other areas of

As a tribute to some of the greatest scientific minds in history, a 1993 episode of *Star Trek* featured Stephen Hawking and actors playing Albert Einstein and Isaac Newton.

physical science has been drastically reduced. A good example is the cancellation in 1995 by the U.S. Congress of the huge particle collider, the Superconducting Supercollider (SSC), which was being constructed in Texas.

Hawking has done as much as any other living scientist to create or increase public interest in the science of cosmology. Whether this interest will result in public financial support for the type of expensive research that will answer the outstanding questions of cosmology remains to be seen. Without this public interest, however, it seems certain that progress in this area will go much more slowly than it has during the past half century.

Stephen Hawking has also played a major role in stimulating public interest in exploring the connection between religion and scientific cosmology. He has urged cosmologists to examine the very instant of the creation, if creation there was, of the universe itself. He has equated the achievement of a complete physical theory to knowing "the mind of God." Paul Davies, who won the 1995 Templeton Prize for Progress in Religion, used Hawking's phrase as the title for one of his several books comparing scientific and religious cosmology.

In this age of change and anxiety, Hawking's speculations about the relationship of a creator to the universe may seem especially challenging, even threatening. Some would argue that scientists should leave certain questions—for example, how the universe began—to the theologians (specialists in the study of religion). History shows, however, that science inevitably expands its domain, even against the toughest opposition. Brilliant people like Hawking show us the scientific views of things. We can then integrate these views with our own religious and philosophical values to find meaning in our own lives, and perhaps even in the universe.

An Inspiration for the Intellect

Many people think that Stephen Hawking is inspirational simply because of his persistent struggle against ALS. But what is truly inspirational about his story is his persistent struggle to understand the cosmos. Consider the leaps of imagination required to ascend from our familiar world to a view of the origin of the universe. It is true that Hawking has not leaped up from ground zero—Einstein made that leap, and Hawking is part of a community of cosmologists, many of whom have made important contributions. But Hawking has distinguished himself by the altitude he has reached. Perhaps, through his engaging writings and the fascinating insights they provide into the workings of his powerful intellect, we and generations to come will be inspired to study cosmology and complete Hawking's quest.

Glossary

absorption spectrum A spectrum indicating the amount of light absorbed by a given substance or object in a given region of the electromagnetic spectrum.

ALS Amyotrophic lateral sclerosis. A progressive and debilitating disease that destroys the nerves that carry messages from the brain to the muscles. Often called Lou Gehrig's disease.

antiparticle A particle identical but opposite in charge and other qualities to a particular normal particle of matter. When a particle and antiparticle come into contact, they annihilate each other, leaving only energy.

astronomy The science of the bodies that can be observed in the heavens.

astrophysicist A scientist who studies the laws of physics governing objects in the heavens.

atmosphere A deep layer of gas surrounding the surface of a star or planet.

atom The smallest particle of a chemical element that has all the chemical properties of the element. An atom consists of a nucleus surrounded by one or more electrons.

baby universe A small, self-contained universe that grows out of a singularity in another universe.

Big Bang theory The theory that the universe—and all of its space, time, matter, and energy—began with an explosion between 10 billion and 20 billion years ago.

black hole A region of space-time in which gravity is so strong that neither electromagnetic radiation nor matter can escape from it (except via the process of Hawking radiation).

chemical composition The chemical substances (and possibly their relative amounts) making up a body.

collapsing star A star that gets smaller as its particles move closer together.

cosmology The study of the origin and structure of the universe as a whole.

density The mass (quantity of matter) in a given volume divided by the volume.

electromagnetic radiation Light and other forms of radiation that travel at the speed of light through space from their source in the form of disturbances in electrical and magnetic fields filling space.

electron An extremely lightweight, pointlike particle with a negative charge. Electrons, whose flowing through wires constitutes current electricity, are found in atoms.

elementary particle A particle that is currently believed to be indivisible into smaller particles.

energy In physics, the ability to do work or cause change. Forms of energy include light and other forms of electromagnetic radiation, heat, the energy of moving bodies, sound, and even (according to the special theory of relativity) mass.

entropy A measure of the randomness of the matter and/or energy contained in a given region of space-time. According to the second law of thermodynamics, the entropy of the universe always increases.

Euclidean space-time Space-time that has four equivalent (spacelike) dimensions.

event horizon The boundary of a black hole.

evolution A process of change in a certain direction. According to the theory of biological evolution, species change through variation and natural selection.

force In physics, a push or a pull.

galaxy Any of the largest groupings of stars held together by their mutual gravitational attraction.

general relativity Short for "general theory of relativity."

general theory of relativity Albert Einstein's theory based on the assumption that the laws of physics should be the same for all observers regardless of their motion. According to this theory, gravitation results from distortions in four-dimensional space-time and affects the measurements of time and distance.

gravitational attraction The tendency of bodies to move toward each other as a consequence of the amount of matter that they contain.

gravitational collapse The collapse of an object into a smaller volume as a consequence of the gravitational attraction between its parts.

gravitational energy The potential energy a body has because of its position as compared to other bodies.

Hawking radiation The elementary particles and electromagnetic radiation emitted from the event horizons of black holes.

Law of Conservation of Matter A physical law that states that matter is never created or destroyed. Since the discovery that matter and energy can be converted to each other, this law has been replaced by a more general "law of conservation of matter and energy."

light Electromagnetic radiation that can be detected by our eyes and hence is responsible for our sense of sight.

light-year The distance light travels through outer space in one year; this distance is estimated to be approximately 6 trillion miles.

mass Quantity of matter.

matter Anything that has weight and occupies space.

mechanics A branch of physics that deals with the forces and energy involved with moving bodies.

mini black holes Subatomic-size black holes (with masses the size of Earth mountains) that formed shortly after the Big Bang.

neutron A heavy, uncharged particle in the nucleus of an atom. Neutrons typically are about half of the total number of particles in an atomic nucleus.

no-boundary model of the universe The idea that the universe is finite in extent but has no boundaries or edges and no beginning in imaginary time.

nuclear Relating to the nucleus of an atom.

nuclear fusion The joining of two atomic nuclei to form a heavier nucleus.

nucleus, nuclei The singular and plural forms, respectively, of the dense central portion of an atom. Atomic nuclei are made of protons and neutrons.

particle accelerators Machines that accelerate charged subatomic particles to extremely high speeds and then cause them to crash into each other or into stationary targets. These collisions often produce new types of subatomic particles.

particle physicist A physicist who studies subatomic particles.

photon A quantum particle of light or other form of electromagnetic radiation.

proton A heavy nuclear particle with a positive charge; the number of protons in an atomic nucleus determines the chemical and physical properties of the corresponding chemical element.

quantum cosmology Cosmological theory based on

applying quantum mechanical techniques to space-time itself.

quantum gravity The laws of physics resulting from combining general relativity with quantum mechanics.

quantum mechanics The theory that describes the behavior of very small objects such as molecules, atoms, and subatomic particles.

quark A charged elementary particle that is a component of protons, neutrons, and other subatomic particles influenced by the strong nuclear force.

radiation Any form of high-speed particles or rays.

red shift A shift in the lines in an electromagnetic spectrum to longer wavelengths due to the motion of the source of the radiation away from the observer.

singularity A point in space-time at which (according to the general theory of relativity) the curvature of the space-time is infinitely great so that ordinary laws of physics break down.

space-time The four-dimensional "environment" for the universe's contents, resulting from the unification of space and time according to Einstein's special theory of relativity.

space-time singularity See singularity.

special theory of relativity Einstein's theory based on the assumption that the laws of physics should be the same for all observers that are not accelerating, no matter how fast they are moving. According to this theory, 1) light travels at the same speed for every observer, 2) nothing can travel faster than the speed of light, 3) an object's mass increases and its length along the direction of its motion decreases as it accelerates, 4) mass and energy can be converted to each other, and 5) events that are simultaneous for one observer are not simultaneous for a second observer moving with respect to the first observer.

spectral lines Bright lines in an emission spectrum that were emitted by specific incandescent elements or dark lines in an otherwise continuous spectrum resulting from the absorption of light by specific "cool" elements.

spectrum The distribution of wavelengths over which electromagnetic waves can exist ranging from gamma rays (short wavelengths) to radio waves (long wavelengths). Also, a picture showing the intensity of electromagnetic radiation at different wavelengths throughout a given range, after radiation from a given source has been passed through a prism.

star A celestial object that now produces, or once produced, energy in nuclear reactions occurring at its center.

steady-state theory A theory in astronomy, now generally out of favor, according to which the universe has always existed and has always been expanding, with hydrogen being created continuously such that the overall density of the universe remains the same despite the expansion.

subatomic particles Particles smaller than the atoms of chemical elements.

thermodynamics The branch of physics concerned with the laws governing heat.

uncertainty principle Heisenberg's principle that one can never simultaneously know the precise location and the precise velocity of a particle. The greater the certainty in one of these measurements, the greater the uncertainty in the other.

wave A disturbance that travels through some medium. For example, sound waves can be a disturbance traveling through air.

wormhole A hypothetical thin connection between two different universes or between two widely separated locations in a single universe.

Further Reading

Ardley, Neil. *Light.* New York: Macmillan, 1992.

Bernie, David. *Light.* New York: Dorling Kindersley, 1992.

Challoner, Jack. *Energy.* New York: Dorling Kindersley, 1993.

Cooper, Christopher. *Matter.* New York: Dorling Kindersley, 1992.

Couper, Heather, and Henbest, Nigel. *The Space Atlas: A Pictorial Guide to Our Universe.* Orlando, FL: Harcourt Brace, 1992.

Gribben, John, and Gribben, Mary. *Time and Space.* New York: Dorling Kindersley, 1994.

Henderson, Harry. *The Importance of Stephen Hawking.* San Diego, CA: Lucent Books, 1995.

Lafferty, Peter. *Force and Motion.* New York: Dorling Kindersley, 1992.

Lippincott, Kristen. *Astronomy.* New York: Dorling Kindersley, 1994.

McDaniel, Melissa. *Stephen Hawking: Revolutionary Physicist.* New York: Chelsea House, 1994.

Simon, Sheridan. *Unlocking the Universe: A Biography of Stephen Hawking.* New York: Dillon Press, 1991.

Sources

Boslough, John. *Stephen Hawking's Universe*. New York: Avon, 1985.

Ferguson, Kitty. *Stephen Hawking: Quest for a Theory of Everything*. New York: Bantam, 1992.

Halliwell, Jonathan J. "Quantum Cosmology and the Creation of the Universe." *Scientific American*. December 1991.

Hawking, Stephen. *Black Holes and Baby Universes and Other Essays*. New York: Bantam, 1993.

———. *A Brief History of Time*. New York: Bantam, 1988.

———. *A Brief History of Time: A Reader's Companion*. New York: Bantam, 1992.

———. "The Quantum Mechanics of Black Holes." *Scientific American*. January 1977.

Linde, Andrei. "The Self-Reproducing Inflationary Universe." *Scientific American*. November 1994.

Luminet, Jean-Pierre. *Black Holes*. New York: Cambridge University Press, 1992.

McDaniel, Melissa. *Stephen Hawking: Revolutionary Physicist*. New York: Chelsea House, 1994.

Silk, Joseph. *A Short History of the Universe*. New York: Scientific American Library, 1994.

Thorne, Kip S. *Black Holes and Time Warps: Einstein's Outrageous Legacy*. New York: W.W. Norton, 1994.

Wheeler, John Archibald. *A Journey Into Gravity and Spacetime*. New York: Scientific American Library, 1990.

White, Michael, and Gribben, John. *Stephen Hawking: A Life in Science*. New York: Dutton, 1992.

INDEX

Boldfaced, italicized page numbers include picture references.

Photo Credits
Cover (background): ©R. Russell/Leo de Wys, Inc.; cover (inset) and pages 22, 37, 48, 53, 57, 64, 77, 85, 87, 92, 95, 98: AP/Wide World Photos; page 4: ©Black Star/Romano Cagnoni/PNI; pages 8, 11, 15, 25, 26, 75: ©Manni Mason's Pictures; pages 19, 73: North Wind Picture Archives; page 31: ©Ronald Royer/Science Photo Library/Photo Researchers, Inc.; page 41: The National Baseball Hall of Fame and Museum; page 89: Archive Photos/PA News; page 91: ©David A. Hardy/Science Photo Library/Photo Researchers, Inc.
Artwork by Blackbirch Graphics, Inc.

B
Haw

Cole, Ron.

**Stephen Hawking :
solving the
mysteries of the
universe**